THE LONDON
VOLVO
B9TL AND B5LH

Matthew Wharmby

THE LONDON
VOLVO
B9TL AND B5LH

PEN & SWORD
TRANSPORT
AN IMPRINT OF PEN & SWORD BOOKS LTD.

Matthew Wharmby

Contents

Cover: **VW 1039 (LK10 BXG) was one of Metroline's first Volvo B9TLs, operating from Brentford on the E2 and E8, and on 22 April 2018, having had a refurbishment, is seen at Ealing Broadway.** *Author*

Back cover, top left: **Go-Ahead took to the B9TL with gusto; WVL 290 (LX59 CZG) was new for the 21 at London Central's New Cross but on 9 March 2017 is seen at East Greenwich on the 129.** *Author*

Back cover, top right: **Stagecoach remained firmly wedded to the Enviro400 but took two batches of Volvo B5LHs, the second with Alexander Dennis bodywork for the 47. 13102 (BL65 OYY) is leaving the much-revamped Lewisham area on 13 August 2017.** *Author*

Back cover, bottom left: **The aesthetics of Wright's Gemini 3 redesign were contentious in the extreme, but sales have continued. Arriva London North won the 19 in 2017 and use examples like Tottenham's HV 274 (LK17 AFF) at Hyde Park Corner on 24 September 2017.** *Author*

Back cover, bottom right: **Egyptian-based MCV added its EvoSeti bodywork to the UK range available for the Volvo B5LH and Tower Transit took 51 like Westbourne Park's MV 38202 (LJ17 WRC), seen at Golders Green on 25 February 2018 on the recast 13.** *Author*

Title page: **The 19 spent five years with London General, shared between Stockwell and Northumberland Park; WVL 482 (LJ61 NWU) at the Angel on 9 July 2015 is one of the latter's.** *Author*

First published in Great Britain in 2020 by Pen and Sword Transport
An imprint of
Pen & Sword Books Ltd
Yorkshire - Philadelphia

Copyright © Matthew Wharmby, 2020

ISBN 978 1 52674 963 5

The right of Matthew Wharmby to be identified as Author of this work has been asserted by him in accordance with the Copyright, Designs and Patents Act 1988.

A CIP catalogue record for this book is available from the British Library.

Typeset by Matthew Wharmby

Printed and bound in China through Printworks Global Ltd.

Pen & Sword Books Ltd incorporates the Imprints of Pen & Sword Books Archaeology, Atlas, Aviation, Battleground, Discovery, Family History, History, Maritime, Military, Naval, Politics, Railways, Select, Transport, True Crime, Fiction, Frontline Books, Leo Cooper, Praetorian Press, Seaforth Publishing, Wharncliffe and White Owl.

For a complete list of Pen & Sword titles please contact

PEN & SWORD BOOKS LIMITED
47 Church Street, Barnsley, South Yorkshire, S70 2AS, England
E-mail: enquiries@pen-and-sword.co.uk
Website: www.pen-and-sword.co.uk

or

PEN AND SWORD BOOKS
1950 Lawrence Rd, Havertown, PA 19083, USA
E-mail: Uspen-and-sword@casematepublishers.com
Website: www.penandswordbooks.com

Foreword

Despite its status as one of the two major suppliers of London's buses in the last two decades, Volvo stumbled after the immensely successful B7TL. Due to the insistence on lowering emissions at the expense of performance, the smaller turbocharged engines specified in the B7TL were overworked and the noise they put out became overwhelming, to the extent that Transport for London objected and effectively banned the model until Volvo had sorted out the noise problems.

Volvo rose to the challenge and unveiled the B9TL, quickly winning back customers that had defected to Alexander Dennis's Enviro400, successor to the Trident. In five years more than 700 B9TLs had entered service in London, all bodied by Wrightbus save for three Enviro400s and two MCW-bodied demonstrators.

Continuing legislation prompted the development of battery-hybrid double-deckers, and in response to this imperative Volvo developed the B5LH, which became more popular still, to the extent that there are now more B5LHs in service than there are diesel B9TLs. Ordered and put into service by all of the main TfL contractors, the B5LH is bodied predominantly by Wrightbus but latterly has seen participation by Alexander Dennis and MCV.

Advancing developments into rechargeable electric technology have, as it has turned out, caught Volvo rather short, as London companies' orders for the B5LH paused by the middle of 2018, forming a perfect spot at which to break this narrative summing up the first decade of the B9TL and B5LH; however, these vehicles and what follow in electric form will be Volvo's double-deck flagship in London for the rest of the decade and into the next.

Matthew Wharmby
Walton-on-Thames, July 2018

Left: **As the Volvo B9TL gave way to the hybrid B5LH, what 'London' uniqueness they had gradually seeped away. With few exceptions, later deliveries were registered by the manufacturers, and as Volvo's reception centre is in the West Midlands, these ostensibly London buses all carried Birmingham registrations, like Stagecoach Selkent's 13016 (BN14 WAO) on the 53 at Westminster on 20 November 2014. These buses were later ousted from the flagship 53 by E40H MMCs and now work on routes more local to their operating Plumstead garage.** *Author*

Go-Ahead London

B, VE, WVL, WHV, EHV, MHV, WVN and VHP classes

Below: **To all intents and purposes B 9 (BX06 BTF) looked just like a WVL, but for the two additional intakes on the side, one of which was for the AdBlue fuel additive. Allocated to Putney in this 24 May 2008 shot, it is seen on the 74 at Marble Arch.**
Author

Surprise was the order of the day when on 4 July 2006 London General took delivery of BX06 BTF, a Volvo B9TL demonstrator with Wrightbus Gemini H41/21D bodywork. Identical to existing company WVLs and carrying the same livery, the bus was to Euro 4 emissions standards, which it was hoped had cut down noise problems sufficient to attract the large and regular orders needed from London bus companies. It was numbered B 9 for the duration and went into service at Stockwell on 18 July; its intended home was on the 11 but it was quickly tried out on the 87, 133 and 196. After nearly a year's service

it returned to Volvo in June 2007, but came back that December and resumed service on the 11.

Thanks to experience with B 9, Go-Ahead ordered three Volvo B9TLs on 10 January 2008, but these would be Alexander Dennis Enviro400-bodied as the VE class. They would be put into service on the 85 to strengthen the company's bid to retain the route, and to get Putney's drivers ready for them, B 9 was transferred from Stockwell late in January and began working on the 74.

The 85 was duly retained and given a three-bus boost to its PVR perfect to accomodate

Left: **Elegantly proportioned and attractive in a discreet sort of way, the Enviro400 body sat well on the Volvo B9TL chassis, though, as it happened, Go-Ahead would not order any more of this combination and neither would anyone else. The 85 had in latter years been projected south from its modern terminus at Fairfield Road in Kingston to stand in Kingston Hall Road, which is where Putney's VE 3 (LX58 CWM) is seen heading when captured on 4 May 2010.** *Author*

the new VEs, which arrived at Volvo's Beddington premises during September and were taken into stock in October.

To H41/24D plus 20 standing, VEs 1-3 were powered by Volvo D9C engines mated to Voith D864 transmission. All three went into service on the 85 on 13 October, though were taken out of traffic two days later and only returned after several weeks, once modifications had been made to the engine cooling grilles at the rear. While at Putney appearances were possible on the 14. Once the VEs were in service and trusted enough

to stay that way, B 9 was returned to Volvo, formally leaving fleet strength by the end of 2008. It later was evaluated (though not in service) by Arriva London North in advance of their own orders for B5LH hybrids.

All in all, the B9TL had proven a success with Go-Ahead, and volume orders could now commence. By the summer of 2009, routes 21 and 63 had been retained by London Central on the promise of new buses and an order was placed in August for sixty Wright-bodied Volvo B9TLs. However, rather than carry on the B code of their predecessor,

Left: **The rear of the Enviro400 body on Volvo B9TL chassis was less tidy, with more grilles needed to counter the threat of overheating posed by underpowered turbocharged engines; the noise problem that this created had cost Volvo three years' worth of orders that it was desperate to remedy. On 11 August 2012 VE 3 (LX58 CWM) sets off from Putney Bridge Station.** *Author*

the new buses were appended to the WVL class despite having different chassis, thus becoming WVLs 274 up.

Accordingly, a refresh was carried out front and rear, the elegant round headlights of the Gemini being replaced by a rather more protruding front, albeit with a chrome-edged faux grille which couldn't be painted over, as had ruined the external appearance of so many of the original Geminis. Go-Ahead's latest interior was featured, with its dark blue seats and blue interior walls, while at the front a striped effect was applied to the entrance doorway to make it more visible to the partially sighted.

First to assume its new contract was the 21 on 10 October 2009, with the 63 following on 14 November. Their outer counterparts 321 and 363 had also been included in each parent's respective tendering scheme and won by the incumbent but with existing PVLs refurbished rather than new B9TLs. The new buses would also take over the N21 and N63 at night.

It had been the intention for a long time to introduce some sort of advanced operation to the Barking-Thames View Estate corridor, but as budgetary concerns made themselves felt this was downgraded from trams to trolleybuses to plain buses, and in the summer of 2009 the network was formalised as East London Transit, replacing the 369 and incorporating an extension along unserved Choats Road to Dagenham Dock station. Under the number (for the moment) of TG1, the route was awarded to Blue Triangle at Rainham, Go-Ahead's representative in the sector, and sixteen more Wright-bodied Volvo B9TLs were ordered. To make up for their being not appreciably different from regular buses, they would be given a special livery of red with orange accents and unique moquette, and stops and shelters along the corridor would be redesigned in the same manner, all in time for a forecast February 2010 start.

Prior to delivery WVL 275 was exhibited at Wright's stand at Bus & Coach at the NEC on 7/8 October; at 10.404m long and 4.395m tall, its unladen weight was 12110 kg. Power was by Volvo's D9B engine mated to a ZF Ecolife six-speed gearbox. Similar, but rather heavier VN 37788 for First was displayed on Volvo's stand. After that, WVLs 274 onward started arriving in October. As well as the redesign of front and rear, the proportion of metal to glass was also altered at the end of each deck so that the rearmost window was curtailed. Weight problems had been as much an issue with modern buses as the noise they emitted,

Right: **Maybe less attractive than the original Gemini, the Gemini 2 nonetheless featured modern aesthetics like small LED-powered headlights, and the W-shaped faux grille with its chrome edging was a reminder of who built it. On 18 October 2010 New Cross's WVL 281 is seen laying over at the 21's stand behind the Lewisham Centre.** *Author*

Left: **The rear of the Gemini 2 body remained upright by comparison with the front, and in fact was almost square. WVL 286 (LX59 CZC) out of New Cross was making a visit to the otherwise PVL-operated 36 when sighted at Vauxhall on 13 February 2011.** *Author*

and again high hopes were held that these would be addressed to the satisfaction of TfL and Volvo alike. WVLs 274-302 were for New Cross and, after staging through intermediate storage locations, the first was sighted on the 21 on 2 November and all were in service by the end of the month barring WVL 299, which had been damaged on delivery. As was New Cross's forte, they could soon be seen straying to the 36, 171, 172 and 321.

Peckham's now followed, comprising WVLs 303-333 and going into service on the 63 from 2 December until the last one was delivered in late January 2010, replacing the 2000-vintage AVLs. As well as their intended route, they wandered to the 37 and 363.

East London Transit was scheduled to commence on 20 February 2010 and its Volvo B9TL complement comprised WVLs 334-349. The routes were now known as EL1 and

Below: **Peckham's WVL contingent entered service on the 63 at the end of 2010, and here at the Elephant & Castle on 24 September 2011 is WVL 312 (LX59 CZY).** *Author*

Right: **Visits by the 21's WVLs to the 171 at New Cross are personified here by WVL 287 (LX59 CZD) at Camberwell Green on 19 July 2014.** *Author*

Right: **Blue Triangle's WVL fleet for the East London Transit EL1 and EL2 were delivered in a livery that was also featured prominently on publicity and on the specially-constructed bus stop shelters. Perhaps its only drawback was that it inhibited advertisements and thus revenue, as on WVL 348 (LX59 DFJ) at Barking on 7 July 2013.** *Author*

Right: **The EL2 broke new ground along previously-unserved Choats Road to terminate at Dagenham Dock station. There was no housing around there at the moment, but all that was set to change. On 3 July 2011 Rainham's WVL 342 (LX59 DFA) is picking up at Ilford.** *Author*

EL2, and while the former replaced the 369 outright, plus the 179 south of Ilford, the EL2 provided the projection to Dagenham Dock. Both ran through the otherwise pedestrianised section of Barking High Street, leading to a handful of accidents. Rainham was the operating garage.

In June 2010 London Central was awarded back its own 229 and 422 on the promise of new buses. Not that the existing 2000-vintage PVLs were anywhere close to worn out, and even less so since they'd been refurbished, but events were again to fall in Volvo's favour with an order placed for 36 more WVLs. Contract start date was 22 January 2011.

London Central wasn't the only Go-Ahead firm that had helped to get Volvo's double-deck manufacturing business going again; in the last third of July the company sent two examples to Brighton & Hove to evaluate what it might like to purchase next after all-Polish Scanias. First came E 35 and next WVL 310, and it was experience of the latter that prompted volume orders for Volvo chassis.

Although tendering had cost London Central the 172 in July, the company would retain both the 12 and 171 when another tranche was announced in September. At the same time the 474, operating out of the Silvertown depot of Docklands Buses, was retained with an element of new vehicles to replace its PVLs. Now that Volvo was on the point of putting the B5LH hybrid into production, and mindful of the coming desire by TfL to tackle emissions in central London, an order for the 12 was delayed until it was determined what proportion of its PVR could be converted to hybrids and which undertaking would fund such a move. For the moment, the stock for the 171 and the partial allocation to the 474, retained at the same time would be made up of, was made up of 36 more B9TLs (WVLs 387-421).

Bexleyheath's new fleet, WVL 350-385, were in build from November and started to arrive in late December, first going into store at Belvedere. The contract change date for the 229 and 422 was 22 January 2011 but examples began entering service on the 6th. Naturally they were soon seen on the 89, 321, 401, 486 and 669.

On 6 March London Central lost the 172 to Abellio, precluding the appearance of any more WVLs. The 171's batch, meanwhile, was

Below: **Thirty-six WVLs went into service at Bexleyheath at the beginning of January 2011. On 30 July at Woolwich we can see WVL 357 (LX60 DWG).** *Author*

attracting attention from elsewhere, WVL 406 paying a visit to Dublin during February in the interest of Dublin Bus resuming dual-doored operation in that city. After a period in store, they began reaching the capital late in March, in advance of the 30 April contract date for both routes 171 and 474. After preparation at Belvedere, New Cross's new WVLs began hitting the streets on 4 April and soon mixing themselves up with the 21's batch and vice versa. The 474's nine followed, assembling at Silvertown from the 16th and going into service from the 21st, alongside the existing SO-class Scanias. Within a few weeks they were regular sightings on the 425 and even on the 150 school bus.

It was now time to order the buses for the conversion of the 12 from artics back to double-deck after an ignominious seven years following its last RMLs. Hybrid technology had now advanced sufficient for Volvo to offer its B5LH for orders; this battery-electric

bus's engine would switch off when at a stop, only to cut back in seconds thereafter using stored energy from braking. Sixteen formed part of the order for the 12, commencing new WHV class. The balance for that route was made up of 33 more WVLs, incorporating a further number for the D7, which was the double-deck element of a clean sweep by Docklands Buses of routes operating in the Isle of Dogs peninsula. There was a caveat, unfortunately, in that the elegant London Central livery of black window surrounds and charcoal grey skirt was ordered deleted for dreary all-red, and the changeover would fall at some point during this run.

MCV had now developed its double-deck body for the Volvo B9TL, and a demonstrator was taken on loan by Go-Ahead London from 20 May. Classified VM 1 and registered BJ11 XGZ, its unladen weight was a hefty 12373 kg, and on 1 June it entered service on the 474 from Docklands Buses' Silvertown garage. On the 7th it was returned to MCV for rectification work and stayed there until 29 July, after which it turned out on the 425 and 474 as fit.

4 June saw the 129 won by London Central with ED-class Darts from New Cross, but the garage's WVLs started making appearances as early as 10 June.

June saw a valuable tender award which would bring the 19 and 249 back to London General from March 2012; in August their vehicle complement was firmed up as an all-Volvo batch of 20 WVLs and 16 WHVs. Go-Ahead-affiliated Blue Triangle was awarded

the 20 in July for similar takeup the following March.

On the evening of Monday 8 August civil disturbance swept various areas of inner London, and WVL 302 as NX73 on the 171 found itself caught in the mayhem. It was set on fire and its body burnt to the chassis, but the vehicle itself would prove salvageable.

Go-Ahead's orders from now until March 2012 comprised 312 vehicles, and the first to arrive were the D7's thirteen intended

Above: **The 171's proper batch of WVLs are represented at Waterloo on 25 May 2013 by New Cross's WVL 398 (LX11 CVZ).** *Author*

Below: **And the rear aspect, demonstrated by WVL 407 (LX11 CWM) at Holborn on 11 June 2011.** *Author*

WVLs during August, Unfortunately, after a truly valiant period of holding out, Go-Ahead had now been compelled to have its new stock delivered in dreary all-red, and the changeover applied from WVL 422. The D7 was assumed on 17 September and together with the input of single-deck routes D6 and D8 on the same day, made for a considerable expansion of Silvertown's operations. VM 1 soon racked up appearances on the D7.

WHVs 1 and 2 staged through Heysham docks on 12 September as the vanguard of the 12's hybrid batch; its WVLs were delivered during the same month and WHV 13 was an exhibit at Coach & Bus on 5/6 October. In fact the WVLs started entering service early when, beginning on 23 September, they were put into traffic on the 45 so that its PVLs could be loaned to Mandela Way to start off the 453 upon its conversion from artic to double-deck the following day, seeing as not all that route's intended new Es had yet arrived. Despite being B9TLs to Camberwell's existing B7TLs, they wandered to the 68; meanwhile, WVL 446 found itself loaned to Rainham for use on the EL1 and EL2 until 4 November.

The 12 duly shed its bendy-buses on 5 November, and that was the end of the type within Go-Ahead. The new Volvos were joined on the first day by WVLs 380-385 transferred from Bexleyheath where they were replaced by six new Es, and thus saw that the grey-skirted livery would have a small presence on the 12.

Left: **Prior to the conversion of the 12 from MAL artic to double-deck, some of the early-arriving WVLs got in some time on the 45 out of Camberwell, as demonstrated on 24 September 2011 by WVL 449 (LJ61 GWK) coming up to the Elephant & Castle.** *Author*

Left: **And as intended on the 12, WVL 435 (LJ61 GWU) passing through Peckham on 14 April 2013.** *Author*

Left: **Exemplifying the growing proportion of hybrid buses with each major conversion, Camberwell's B5LH WHV 3 (LJ61 GVY) circumnavigates Trafalgar Square (in fact, more of a roundabout since the ill-starred road layout changes of 2002). The almost comically short wheelbase and giant overhang is in evidence here.** *Author*

Right: **The 12's fleet was made up by the transfer of the highest-numbered six WVLs from Bexleyheath, allowing (when lucky shots like this permitted) comparison between their discreet and elegant livery and the letdown that was all-red. Camberwell's WVLs 385 (LX60 DXT) and 447 (LJ61 GWF) are caught at the top of Regent Street on 15 June 2014.**
Author

Below: **In return, the all-red livery infiltrated Bexleyheath in the shape of two new deliveries, one of which was WVL 455 (LJ61 GVP) seen at Woolwich on 10 May 2014.**
Author

Of the incoming new buses, WVLs 455 and 456 arrived on 21 December and were nominally for school route 658 at Bexleyheath from January. Although the other schools routes taken up by the garage were furnished by examples of the B7TL variant of the WVL class transferred in, WVL 379 moved over the river to assist Rainham on the EL1 and EL2 for a spell.

March 2012 proved particularly busy for Go-Ahead; on the 24th the 20 was taken up by Blue Triangle using WVLs 457-467. The 19 (including N19) and 249 passed to London General on the 31st; the former was put into Stockwell with WVLs 481-495 and WHVs 17-30, and the latter took up at Merton with WVLs 468-480. A considerable amount of route reallocation had to be executed to clear

Left: **On 24 March 2012 the 20 passed on tender to Go-Ahead with WVL operation from Rainham. Here at Loughton station on the 25th is WVL 458 (LJ61 NUO).** *Author*

Left: **The 19 formed a major win for Go-Ahead, with B9TLs like Stockwell-allocated WVL 489 (LJ61 NWB), in New Oxford Street on 11 August 2012, sharing the route with WHVs.** *Author*

Left: **The 19's B5LH hybrid component is illustrated on 27 May 2012 by Stockwell's WHV 23 (LJ61 NVK), making its way across the recently-constructed Holborn contraflow that enabled this route (and the 38 and 242) to shave a couple of minutes off the time taken to circumnavigate Red Lion Square.** *Author*

the space at Merton and Stockwell for the two new acquisitions. But it was on the 31st that a spectacular coup brought Go-Ahead a whole new garage; this was Northumberland Park (NP), acquired from FirstGroup which was flat broke and wished to pull out of London altogether, accomplishing it in stages. First London had been an early and satisfied customer for the same combination of Volvo B9TL and Wrightbus Gemini 2 body, but had classified their examples VNs. Rather than appending them to the existing WVL class, London General (under whom Northumberland Park was placed, despite it being right across town from their geographical heartland) instituted a new WVN class that comprised 53 buses. With them came routes 259, 357 and 476, though they were also capable of working the 67, 191, 231 and school routes 616, 692 and 699.

Left: **The 357's small batch also made the move to Go-Ahead; Birmingham-registered WVN 47 (BL61 ACX) at Walthamstow Central on 11 August 2012, was formerly known as VN 37945.**
Author

Below: **New as VN 37813, Northumberland Park's WVN 10 (LK59 FEH) is swinging into the one-way system round King's Cross on 27 May 2012.**
Author

Physical renumbering was a slower process, the new numbers only being in evidence from late April onwards and fleetnames a month after that. All were done by the summer.

Meanwhile, Go-Ahead had retained the 22, seven years after its conversion to OPO, and in March ordered its fleet; there would be 13 WVLs and 10 WHVs.

Workings of the B9TL WVLs away from their routes were comparatively rare, but spring 2012 saw sporadic appearances of the 19's WVLs on the 24, while Camberwell put a WHV out on the X68 in July and WVL 479 appeared on the 155 on 15 August. Fire-gutted WVL 302 had been repaired by Wrights in Ballymena and returned to London on 30 May.

A new craze in London, or at least one revived using modern methods, was the all-over advert bus, and in May WVL 276 was the first Go-Ahead B9TL to receive one, for Visa. Despite not extending to include the front, the effect was striking and many

Above: **One of Putney's new WHVs delivered in October 2012, WHV 34 (LJ62 KHV) was later treated to a rear ad for Wicked Uncle, a retailer of gifts, and when captured on 16 October 2014 was crossing Putney Bridge, actually on the 22 for which it was purchased rather than on the 74, which became the class's de facto home.** *Author*

Below: **WHV 36 (LJ62 KGG) was also wearing a rear ad when sighted at Marble Arch on 11 May 2015.** *Author*

more buses of all types and at most other London companies would follow; the extra revenue was that much appreciated! They were returned to red during October and November, during which month a new campaign began for Apple's iPod; WVLs 484 and 488 were two chosen.

For the duration of Olympics season Bexleyheath loaned WVLs 455 and 456 to Silvertown to provide extras on its 425 close to the Olympic Park at Stratford. WVLs 274, 275 and 277 joined 276 in Visa livery during July, in time to tout the brand across London to the large numbers arriving to watch the Olympics (if, that is, they could get tickets!)

WVLs 496-508 would prove to be Go-Ahead's last Volvo B9TLs as most route renewals in central London from 2013 onwards would take place using the New Bus for London, or Borismaster. The 22's new stock needed to be delivered by 13 October in order to displace 05-reg WVLs via refurbishment to Northumberland Park for the 257, and then take up their own renewed contract on the 20th. The WVLs began working out of Putney on the 11th, but right at the death, plans changed when it was pointed out by emissions campaigners (the latest single issue impeding bus operations in London!) that Putney High Street had a consistently high pollution index and that the new buses would be better served on the 74, which served this thoroughfare at least in part while the 22 skirted it. The late delivery of the rest saw sale-bound PVLs reactivated to fill in at Putney, and in any case, within a year the new buses had soon made their home on all of Putney's routes, comprising the 14, 85 and 430.

WVLs 484 and 488 regained red livery in December, and thereafter the fleet of B9TLs and B5LHs entered a very quiet period, with all in place on their assigned routes for the most part and the only changes being to advert liveries. In April 2013 Putney's WHV 39 gained a scheme for Royal Brunei Airlines.

Below: **As sure as dammit, the WVLs ordered against the 22 but subsequently put into service on the 74 would make their way to Putney's other routes sooner or later; here crossing Putney Bridge on 16 October 2014 is WVL 496 (LJ62 KXX) on the 14.** *Author*

On 1 June the 249 was reallocated from Merton to Stockwell, taking with it WVLs 468-480 and adding them to the 19's own pool; but on the 22nd of that month a more significant reallocation was of the 20 from Blue Triangle's Rainham to Northumberland Park so that Blue Triangle could incorporate the last of the First London acquisitions. Northumberland Park was somewhat closer to the 19's line of route, buses coming off service at Finsbury Park being able to just charge up the Seven Sisters Road and through the Tottenham Hale one-way system; with it went WVLs 457-467, which, after fitment of common blinds, could now pop up on the garage's WVN-operated routes.

In June Camberwell's WHV 10 and Putney's WHV 41 received all-over ads for Lycamobile. VM 1 last saw service on 25 July and was returned to Volvo, together with the other VM 1, an identical MCV-bodied B9TL operating with London United.

September saw Camberwell's WHV 13 given an ad for the Burj Khalifa in Dubai. Stockwell's modern Volvos did their share of wandering over the summer, with its WHVs drifting to the 88 and its WVLs to the 196 and 337.

During October a new Volvo B5TL with Wright Gemini 3 body to a substantially revised design was taken on loan, the vehicle having arrived in England through Heysham docks on 8 September. Registered BF63 HFE,

it was classified V 6 for the duration of its stay. Due to revised construction methods adapted from the Borismaster, over a ton's weight saving was achieved over the comparable Gemini 2 and this manifested physically through much smaller windows. Its billed capacity was H41/22D plus 37 standees, and it was put into service at Camberwell on the 12 (see page 184).

Three WHVs were treated to ads in October; WHV 13 exchanged its Dubai

scheme for one exhorting passengers to Visit Malaysia; WHV 39 also received one of these (ex-Royal Brunei), while WHV 12 became one of 2013's Poppy Appeal buses before switching straight after to one advertising Saxony in Germany. In November a glut of WHV ads saw WHVs 5 and 35 promoting the Asus T-100 laptop, WHVs 32 and 38 joining WHV 12 plugging Saxony and WHVs 20, 23 and 36 Dodo 'Lucky New Year'. WHVs 33 and 37 received this latter ad in December and

WHV 39 resumed red. In January, however, came a more permanent change actually using paint; this was WVL 454, which was now considered a permanent member of the EL1/EL2 fleet at Rainham and deserved the livery to prove it. That month saw nine of the WHVs in advert liveries lose them for all-red again, and WHVs 20 and 38 followed in February. WHV 41 removed itself from consideration on 28 March when it suffered an accident at Putney Bridge Station while on

the 85; it was out of action for four months.

V 6 left in March; two other B5TL prototypes were now in London, operating with Metroline and Arriva London North.

Rio 2 came out in the UK on 4 April 2014 and WHVs 8 and 37 were treated to ads for it, another sequel meriting an advert bus was *Spiderman 2* and this was plugged by WHV 8 from March to May. WHV 40 took an ad for Karen Millen in the same month. All were returned to red in June, and in July WHV 38 started advertising Bulmers cider. August saw WHV 10 given an ad for the Gap.

Derby Day perennial 406F saw WHVs and WVLs feature this year from Putney. Between 14 July and 26 September Putney Bridge was closed and its local routes curtailed; of the WVL and WHV operations at Putney, the 14, 74 and 430 terminated at Putney Bridge Station, with a self-contained section of the 430 coming from Roehampton as normal but standing at Lower Richmond Road.

A second V 6 now appeared; registered BJ14 KTL, it came to London Central in August and was also allocated to Camberwell, again on the 12 but very occasionally visiting the 68. Tendering awards announced during the month won the 432 for Go-Ahead for takeup in 2015 with existing buses.

On 31 August the EL1 and EL2 had a service increase requiring three more buses; WVLs 451-453 were transferred from Silvertown to Rainham and treated to East London Transit livery.

Model David Gandy found himself plastered over bus sides during the autumn of 2014; WHVs 14 and 38 were his hosts from September till November. In October WVL 477 was treated to an ad for the Burj Khalifa, WHV 36 to one for Relish Broadband and WHV 15 became 2014's Poppy Day representative for Go-Ahead.

Although hybrid buses were entering services in larger numbers now that the price differential had come down, there was another way of reducing emissions, and that was the flywheel. WVL 450 was converted and was transferred from Stockwell to Camberwell during July; on 11 November it moved on to Northumberland Park for comparison trials on the 191 with WVN 49.

For the moment, however, hybrid orders were the way of the future, and Go-Ahead set out to add to its B5LH fleet when its Docklands Buses subsidiary was awarded the 135 from Arriva London North in September. Unusually, the bodywork would be from Alexander Dennis this time, with its new MMC body; together they would form

Above: **The 249 had moved from Merton since its acquisition, joining the 19 at Stockwell on 1 June 2013. WVL 469 (LJ12 CHC) was now a Stockwell motor and demonstrates on 4 May 2015 at the top of Anerley Hill.** *Author*

Right: **WVL 380 (LX60 DXM) was another B9TL interloper on the B7TL-operated 468 when sighted at the Elephant on 18 January 2015, but this year would see this cohort of six move to Stockwell for the 432.** *Author*

Left: **Candy Crush, the maddening game, was being advertised on Camberwell's WHV 1 (LJ61 GVW) when this bus was photographed approaching the Elephant & Castle on 6 January 2015. This would be the year that Borismasters took over the 12.** *Author*

the EHV class with a debut order for 16 to be taken in time for the 135's assumption on 23 May 2015.

In December a big push was made by the addictive Candy Crush app game, and seven WHVs were treated, comprising WHVs 1, 2, 5-7, 14 and 15. WHV 15 was the Poppy Day bus, while WHV 10 was red by year's end.

The march of the Borismaster now encompassed the 12, and WVLs and WHVs started departing from 28 March. Camberwell's contingent of 60-reg WVLs (380-385), plus WVLs 436-439, 443 and 444, moved to Stockwell to take over the 432 on 4 April. It was thought at one point that the 432 would be operated with WHVs, but this was changed so as to reflect TfL's near obsession with adding hybrids to as many purely central London routes as possible. To make space available at Stockwell, half the 19 was in turn reallocated, rather surprisingly, to Northumberland Park; WVLs 481-495 made the trip and could be identified on the 19 by their lack of running numbers.

Metrobus now edges into the story. In spite of having been affiliated with Go-Ahead for some time and more recently formally brought closer into integration with London

Left: **Now that Northumberland Park was part of London General it could be put to use taking overspill from its counterpart garages on the other side of town; on 4 April 2015 half the 19 was put in from Stockwell, taking with it sixteen WVLs like WVL 483 (LJ12 CHF) seen in Chelsea on 12 April.** *Author*

General, the company had been a resolute Scania user; it had got rid of its Tridents after one innings and had never dabbled in Volvos, but in December the retention on tender of the 119 and 202 prompted an order for 39 more WHVs to be numbered as such (WHV 42-80) rather than the numeric fleetnumbers used hitherto. Additionally, these would be to the stark and controversial new angular body still, confusingly, called Gemini 3. It was thought at first that these should actually go onto the 14 and displace WVLs for Scania replacement at Metrobus Croydon, but unusually the suburban operations got their way instead.

V 6 was replaced at Camberwell by Streetdeck demonstrator WSD 1 and moved at the end of February to Bexleyheath for

trials on the 229. In February all the Candy Crush WHVs reverted to red save WHV 5, which gained an ad for Peru instead (carried till May); WHV 37 gained an ad for Karen Millen and WVL 477 regained red livery. WHV 36 was restored to red in March.

The balance of the WVLs displaced from the 12 by the incoming Borismasters were parcelled out between Sutton (WVL 441), New Cross (WVLs 442 and 446) Peckham (WVL 445) and Northumberland Park (WVLs 448 and 449) as top-ups.

Above: **The 12's outgoing WVLs were apportioned out where needed; Northumberland Park got two of them and here at Edmonton Green on 19 December 2015 is WVL 449 (LJ61 GWK).** *Author*

Left: **Peckham's gift from the Borismaster conversion of the 12 was WVL 445 (LJ61 GWD), which is seen at King's Cross on the morning of 10 June 2015.** *Author*

In April WHV 32 exchanged its Karen Millen ad for one for Crocs shoes. That month saw the second V 6 return to Volvo, its work done but no further B5TLs ordered.

May saw the 155 retained on tender and a second order for new-front Gemini 3 WHVs ordered; enough would be included in this order for thirty (WHV 81-110) to add a proportion to Sutton for the 93 when its own tender was assured the following month.

It was now time to provision the 135, but its EHVs were late arriving so London Central took the opportunity to complete the hybridisation of the 436 by transferring the WHVs down the road to New Cross and thus displace a contingent of Es to Silvertown in time for the 135's 23 May start. The EHVs, in build during May and June, duly made their appearance in June and were put into service beginning on the 18th of that month; the last one was in traffic on 16 July. Inconsistencies in the allocation of registrations were not helped by the modern practice of letting the manufacturers register the vehicles, which not only meant alien marks (in this case, those of Birmingham) appearing on London buses, but in completely random order based on chassis number. In service, as well as the 135 the EHVs would pop up on the D7 from time to time.

Left: **The 12's conversion to Borismaster saw the route's WHVs move down the street to New Cross to render the 436 100% hybrid despite the existing allocation being EHs. On 18 June 2015 WHV 5 (LJ61 GWA), still with Camberwell coding, prepares to enter Vauxhall bus station.** *Author*

Left: **A new class made its debut in 2015 with the Alexander Dennis Enviro400-bodied version of the Volvo B5LH, indistinguishable from its integral counterpart other than the unmistakable short wheelbase. Silvertown had the first EHVs when the 135 was taken over from Arriva London North, and on 10 September EHV 16 (BL15 HBN) is seen passing interminable roadworks at Aldgate.** *Author*

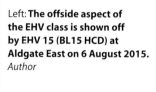

Left: **The offside aspect of the EHV class is shown off by EHV 15 (BL15 HCD) at Aldgate East on 6 August 2015.** *Author*

Above: **Karen Millen-adorned WHV 37 (LJ62 KGN) makes a visit to the 85 at Putney Bridge Station on 27 May 2015.** *Author*

Right: **TfL's own ad extolling the virtues of 1,200 hybrid buses in service by 2015 was carried at one point by Putney's WHV 38 (LJ62 KGY), seen in Putney High Street on 25 June 2015 while visiting the 430.** *Author*

During June WHV 37 lost its Karen Millen ad but WHV 25 gained one for the Sony PS4; in July Crocs WHV 32 reverted to red.

Both buses numbered V 6 may have been disposed of, but Go-Ahead took two of the other B5TLs on loan from Volvo on 29 June; these were Arriva VGD 1 (BF63 HDE) and Metroline VW 1469 (BF63 HDG) and both formed part of Wimbledon Tennis and Hampton Court extras operated from Croydon.

On 8 August the first of Metrobus's new WHVs were delivered to Croydon to commence training in advance of the 119's tender renewal date on 29 August, on which date the night version of the 119 was reallocated at the same time from Orpington to Croydon to match its day counterpart. The contract renewal date of the 202 applied from 19 September, its new buses forming an upgrade from single-deck MANs. The WHVs themselves started entering service on the 202 on 22 August, with the 119 commencing on 1 September and the full complement was in position by 18 November. At the same time the two B5TLs were formally acquired and became WVLs 509 and 510; there were now three distinct Volvo chassis with this class code!

Metrobus's new WHVs were also intended as a minority allocation on routes 293 and 405, but in reality it was the 64 that they visited most frequently, followed by the 127 which already had a bewildering variety of chassis. WHV 52 was lent to Merton in October for training the 155's drivers.

Above and below: **Two of Metrobus's Volvo B5LH deliveries in 2015, WHV 49 (BP15 OLW) passing East Croydon on 2 September, and WHV 70 (BF65 WJO) at Crystal Palace on 18 October.** *Both: Author*

Above: **The WHVs off the 119 and 202 strayed to the 64 while Metrobus still had it, and doing so at East Croydon on 18 November 2015 is Croydon's WHV 78 (BF65 WKD).** *Author*

Below: **Stockwell's 88 was converted from EH to LT in 2015, but until then guests like WHV 17 (LJ61 NVC) were apt to turn out, like this bus is doing at Vauxhall when seen on 18 June 2015.** *Author*

In August Go-Ahead was awarded back the 35 and 40, which had been lost to what was now Abellio in 2009; from the following spring the 345 would go the other way. It was a considerable surprise when the company selected MCV's new EvoSeti for the body on its next 20 Volvo B5LHs. This would inaugurate a new MHV class, and would be combined with an order for 22 more EHs (but now to MMC standard).

A lull in advert application was followed in October by the treatment of WHV 31 to a scheme for Dubai, in the same month as WHV 25 reverted to red. In November WVL 493 received an ad for Hungry House, this lasting until January 2016.

WHVs 82-110 began arriving in November and three were put into use on the 155 on 4 December to kick off the conversion one day ahead of schedule. The registrations were in the by now usual hopeless mess, which perhaps detracted from the extreme harshness of the body design! Instead of adding a full-time Merton allocation to the 93, two journeys were cross-linked from the 155 instead, and it was on one of these journeys that WHV 85 suffered a severe accident on 8 December, its second day in service, which took it off the road for several weeks. The last six of the order went into service at Sutton, commencing on 4 January 2016 with WHV 93, and the balance of Merton's fleet was all in service by the beginning of February. Strange visits at Merton were immediately evident with such a large and diverse runout, and sightings were predominantly on the 270 with occasional visits to the 44, 163 and 280.

In all-over advert terms, the year 2015 ended with WHV 31 regaining red and WHV 40 now plugging Costa Rica. In January WVL 493 returned to all-red.

2016's first order of business was for a number of Bexleyheath WVLs to move out following the loss of the 229 to Arriva on the 23rd, eight going to New Cross, two to Northumberland Park and one to Mandela Way. In February two passed to Camberwell, one to Peckham and one to Stockwell, but that wasn't the end of the type's migration by any means.

On 19 March the East London Transit routes EL1 and EL2 were revised, adding a whopping twelve buses to reflect the EL2's extension to Becontree Heath. To make them all standard, Go-Ahead took WVLs 468-480 out of Stockwell, replacing them on the 249

with the elderly PVLs recently displaced from the 155, and by July repainted them to East London Transit livery. Three staged through Silvertown first. March, however, was more eye-opening in its introduction to Metrobus Croydon of the B9TL version of the WVL. Intended to continue the replacement of the company's Scanias, as B7TL-spec WVLs had already commenced, they joined a miscellany (now including Es!) on the 64, 119, 127, 202 and 405.

30 April was the date of the grand return of the 35 and 40 to Camberwell. The EHs having arrived first, then followed the MCV EvoSeti-bodied MHV class. Even before this new breed of B9TL had gone into service, 65 more were ordered against the tender for the 63, awarded to and retained by London Central in February. They were also to have serviced the simultaneous retention of the 21, but this central London trunk route was now specified for Borismasters and one of a very large tranche of successful tender retentions, the 185, was earmarked instead. These included the 1, 14, 74 and 430, and with Volvo B5LHs sure to form at least part of orders against these contracts, would also see existing WVLs moving to the 132 and 180 in due course. Accordingly, in May 56 more WHVs were ordered (for the 1, 74 and 430), plus 39 EHVs for the 14.

Above: **The need to boost the EL-group forced London General to take WVLs off the 249 and replace them with PVLs ten years their senior. On 29 April 2016, one of the buses in question, former Stockwell WVL 472 (LJ61 NXB), is seen in the otherwise pedestrianised East Street in Barking, on its new deployment to Rainham.** *Author*

Right: **The new MHV class for the 35 and 40 introduced MCV's EvoSeti bodywork to London in strength. The routes returned to Camberwell, from whence they had come in the first place, and at Clapham Common on 4 May 2016 is MHV 5 (BU16 OYN).** *Author*

Purley 127

In April a demonstrator was taken on loan; registered BX14 TJV, it was a B5LH with original-spec Gemini 3 bodywork and had already seen service in Dublin and with National Express West Midlands. It was then formally acquired, taking the number WHV 111 and earmarked for service at Croydon after a spell on Commercial Services work, specifically the Wimbledon Tennis service, then on the Hampton Court flower show and after that, Farnborough.

On 23 June MHV 6 sustained a serious accident with a fire engine while turning into Acre Lane on the 35.

An extensive tendering programme implemented on 2 July took off one route capable of fielding second-generation Volvo low-floor double-deckers (the 85, lost to London United) but substituted two more. The 57 came back to Merton, nominally with Es but also with WVL 442 as a backup transferred from New Cross, whilst the 337 was transferred from Stockwell to Putney to replace the 85, taking its dedicated Es with it but also adding WVL 435. The possibility for Putney's existing B9TL WVLs and WHVs would only come when blinds incorporating Putney's new acquisition were printed later in the year. VEs 1-3 were transferred from Putney to Sutton after the loss of the 85 and put into service on the 213.

Richmond 337

Sky Q. THE NEXT GENERATION BOX

Clapham Park 57

Right: **29 Es into Merton for the 57 were backed up by WVL 440 (LJ61 GWZ), seen in Kingston on 19 October.** *Author*

The 64 was removed from consideration for WHV operation when it was lost to Arriva London South on 27 August; here it was Scanias that were withdrawn.

As the existing MHVs began to wander from the 35 and 40 to the X68, the second batch started arriving, higher numbers first.

MHVs 56-85 were first seen in service on 27 September, within a week being enough in numbers to have taken over the 42 in its entirety in advance of its re-routeing to Dulwich from 1 October (and a good deal in advance of the delivery of its own order for EHs). They were meant for the 185 at

Right: **The 42 was awaiting its own EHs; it was the 185 that the MHVs were meant for, like MHV 67 (BV66 VFZ) at Lewisham on 11 October 2016.** *Author*

Camberwell, but as well as that route and the 42 they mixed with the previous MHV intake on the 35 and 40 plus PVL-operated 45. They also took advantage of the pooled status with Mandela Way, popping up on the 1 (and N1) before its own WHVs arrived. To prepare the garage otherwise, WHV 111 was transferred from Croydon.

On 1 October there was a raft of changes in east London; relevant to the WVLs was the reallocation of the 474 from Silvertown to the new River Road, taking with it WVLs 413-421. The D8 was new to the class, otherwise being double-decked with Scanias ex-Metrobus. Sutton took on six B9TL-based WVLs as general top-ups and refurbishment cover for DOEs, this role having already been undertaken by two most unlikely combinations of Scania chassis; this shuffle also rotated out Merton's WVLs 442 and 444 and replaced them with WVLs 440 and 446.

The Volvo B5LH was undoubtedly popular within London General, but it would not have 2016 all to itself, as the order for EHVs was amended to become Enviro400H-based EHs instead and thus takes itsef out of our story other than by association.

Some new visits during the year were of Merton WHVs to the 118 and Stockwell WHVs to the 196, with WVL 381 on the 170 just once and only as far as Clapham Junction. WHV 7 lost its Doom advert during August, though in general Borismasters were preferred for all-over ad treatment.

Above: **The 474 was reallocated from Silvertown to the new River Road garage on 30 April, taking along its regular WVLs like WVL 416 (LX11 CWY) at Canning Town on 31 october. The new number blinds were intended to be more readable, but look thin and anaemic!** *Author*

Left: **Sutton was the beneficiary of some of the former Bexleyheath 60-reg WVLs, using them (not to mention two strains of Scania) as cover while its DOEs were away for refurbishment. Here in central Sutton on 14 December 2016 is WVL 365 (LX60 DWU).** *Author*

Right: **The 1's batch of fifteen new WHVs is represented at Waterloo on 26 November 2016 by Mandela Way's WHV 156 (BV66 VLJ).** *Author*

Below: **Although the 363 was restocked during the second half of 2016 with its own EHs, it regularly uses the 63's MHVs delivered at the same time, like Peckham-based MHV 27 (BV66 VKT) at Peckham on 26 October.** *Author*

Below right: **Operating where it was intended on 22 November at the Elephant is MHV 31 (BG66 MHZ).** *Author*

The balance of the new EvoSetis, MHVs 21-55, began to appear in October and went into service at Peckham on the 21st, mixing with the thirteen EHs ordered for the 363 and seeing appropriate reciprocation. To allow the placement of a standard T-shaped advert, the small window hitherto blocking the shank was deleted on this batch of MHVs.

On 17 October Mandela Way's dedicated allocation of Volvo B5LHs, WHVs 143-157, began entering service on the 1 and N1. Putney, allocated WHVs 112-142 and 158-167, commenced service on the 30th, and straightaway they were popping up on the 14 and 22 as well as their assigned 74 and 430; the 14's EHs were still awaited.

In September WHV 17 gained an ad for Zoopla.

The 1's conversion from VWL to WHV was completed in November, whilst Peckham's PVLs were displaced from the 363 by the new EHs and MHVs; the WVLs simultaneously dislodged from the 63 migrated to Belvedere to replace the other half of the VWL fleet from

their latter-day home on the 180. Mandela Way's pooled status with Camberwell saw an interesting reciprocation during November when WHVs 144, 145 and 151 turned out on the 35, 40, 42, 45 and 185.

Bus services in central London were increasingly subject to politically-motivated change, and one such arbitrary alteration

Above: **As 2017 followed 2016, the withdrawal of three Putney routes' worth of B7TL-based WVLs was well along; snatching a patch of sunshine outside Putney Bridge Station on 6 January 2017 is WHV 119 (BV66 VHX).** Author

Left: **Representing the new order of Gemini 3 Volvo B5LHs on the 14 is Putney's WHV 132 (BV66 VLF) picking up at South Kensington Station on 7 December 2016.** Author

Above: **Perhaps a little too early for the anticipated demographic, the 436 was rerouted at Vauxhall to Battersea Park Station, which is where New Cross's WHV 4 (LJ61 GVZ) is going when sighted setting off from Lewisham on 26 November 2016.** *Author*

hacked the 436 out of the West End altogether from 19 November and rerouted its northern path to Battersea Park Station instead, trusting that custom intended to fill the forthcoming flats on the old power station's site would follow. The PVR fell by ten without compensation to the main 36, though it must be remembered that the 436 was only instituted in the first place as somewhere to put artics and had become effectively superfluous once the MALs had been replaced.

Right: **The VWLs new to East Thames Buses had now come to the end of their lifespan, and gradually they were replaced; following the 1's conversion to WHV, the 180 at Belvedere took delivery of most of the WVLs displaced from the 63 at Peckham. Here at Woolwich on 26 November is WVL 320 (LX59 DBY).** *Author*

At the very end of 2016 the 21 started taking its agreed allocation of LTs, although entry into service was extremely slow. The outgoing 59-reg WVLs moved across to the 321 (replacing its ageing PVLs).

2017 bowed with a surprise when Peckham and Sutton undertook a vehicle swap in order to fulfil a Mayoral pledge to treat one of a selection of heavily-polluted corridors to 100% hybrid operation; accordingly, the 63 sent all but six of its MHVs to Sutton for the 93, receiving DOEs in exchange. Sutton's new complement soon turned out on the 80, 151, 154 and 213 and at night on the N155.

Right: **WHV 17 (LJ61 NVC) of the 19's contingent at Stockwell was treated to an ad for Zoopla, and on 6 November 2016 has taken it to Finsbury Park.** *Author*

Right: **Following the receipt of Borismasters for the 21, it was a seamless process to let its WVLs transfer to the 321 in replacement of its 52-reg PVLs. The third major revamp of Lewisham in forty years wiped out the existing streets and funnelled westbound buses round a pair of new buildings and out in front of Lewisham DLR station, where New Cross's WVL 288 (LX59 CZF) is seen on 13 August 2017.** *Author*

Right: **Officially restricted to the 93, Sutton's new intake of ex-Peckham MHVs spread their wings as soon as they arrived; here in Eden Street, Kingston as dusk falls on 23 February 2017 is MHV 25 (BV66 VKR).** *Author*

Left: **The lone original Gemini 3-bodied B5LH became WHV 111 (BX14 TJV) and settled in on the 1 out of Mandela Way. On 9 March 2017 it is going round the Elephant & Castle complex in the reverse direction from comparatively recently, the roundabout having been revamped.** *Author*

On 18 February the East London Transit pair with Blue Triangle, already treated to extensions into the growing Barking Reach region, added a third route on 18 February, although for the moment only this new EL3 (ex-387) assumed Borismaster operation.

Even before all of the B7TL variant of the WVL class had been displaced from Putney by the new WHVs and EHs, WVLs 503-506 were transferred to Merton, increasing the B9TL numbers there. This was because not enough SEs had been made available for the 455's intended 4 March assumption date, so SOEs had to come from the 152.

The 101 was taken over from Stagecoach East London on 4 March, gaining Volvo B9TLs (the WVLs dislodged from the EL group but none de-liveried by that date), and on the

Below: **The assumption by Borismasters of the EL group during the first half of 2017 didn't include the application of East London Transit livery, which was taken away by the former WVLs to the 101, assumed on 4 March. Still based at River Road, WVL 474 (LJ61 NXD) sets off from Wanstead on 26 March 2017.** *Author*

25th the 259 at Northumberland Park was lost to Arriva London North. More damaging for Go-Ahead London as a whole were the twin losses of the 19 and 249 on 1 April, although the latter had already been forced to cede its WVLs. When enough Borismasters had been deployed to River Road to start the EL1 in earnest as well as the other two routes, WVLs 334-344 were reallocated to Metrobus Croydon to take over the X26 from Epsom Buses on 15 April. None of them had been repainted out of East London Transit livery, though the process of doing so was beginning at Hants & Dorset Trim; this process would also include upgrading with luggage racks and conversion to single-door. Naturally, one sneaked off the X26 as early as the first day when WVL 337 turned out on the 405.

Only two WVLs (332 and 333) remained at Peckham by February. Two Zoopla ads to revert to red that month were WHVs 17 and 24, WHVs 51 and 61 following in April.

Left: **WVLs 503-506 were transferred from Putney to Merton to give the recently re-acquired 152 help while its intended mix of SOEs and SEs were themselves assisting another new conquest, the 455 out of Metrobus. WVL 506 (LJ62 KDZ) has reached the 152's first eastbound stop at New Malden on 25 April, and proved a lucky break for the photographer as its driver immediately turned its blinds to blank, threw off the passengers that had already boarded and set off out of service! Saying something for the scheduling that day, so had the SOE immediately ahead of it. It returned to Putney in May.**
Author

The 19's discarded WHVs started to drift back during April, mostly on the 88 where LTs could not manage it, or on the 170, but by the end of the month were beginning to gather at Merton for the 280 (though naturally racking up appearances on the 44, 163 and 270). The WVNs ejected from the 259 began going through refurbishment at Hants & Dorset, their own future task to be the takeover of the 131 from London United. Peckham's last two WVLs found themselves transferred away, WVL 332 to Bexleyheath and WVL 333 (the last in service at Peckham on 21 March) to Northumberland Park.

As the 22 was set to be re-routed to terminate at Oxford Circus via Berkeley Square, Go-Ahead ordered vehicles for it in keeping with the Putney High Street emissions zone that had created such havoc earlier in the year. Just to be different, however, they were to be 14 more MHVs, introducing a third type to Putney. The win of the 188 for 11 November implementation prompted an order for 29 WHVs.

The status of Mandela Way as a pool garage ensured that its WHVs for the 1 wandered, making debut appearances at both Camberwell and Peckham in May.

Left: **The WHVs released from the 19 following its loss to Arriva were gradually transferred from Stockwell to Merton for the 280. Here at Tooting Broadway on 18 June, and actually on its intended route, is WHV 18 (LJ61 NVD).**
Author

Right: **Despite TfL's seeming obsession with devastating the choice available to passengers circumnavigating Oxford Street, the changes of 15 July 2017 were rooted in nothing more than stand availability. The falling back of the 137 to Marble Arch freed its stand for a diversion of the 22 to Oxford Circus so that the 3 could take its post at Piccadilly Circus, and on 18 July Putney's WHV 36 (LJ62 KGG) makes a strange sight this far north.** *Author*

Below: **The eight WVLs into Morden Wharf with the 129 carried their running number sequence with them, but WVL 354 (LX60 DWD) isn't carrying one when sighted pulling onto the stand at Greenwich on 13 August. Plans were unveiled at about this point to extend the 129 from Greenwich to Lewisham in place of the 180, in accordance with projections of the likely effect of the opening of the Elizabeth Line.** *Author*

However, on 29 July Mandela Way was closed, but a new site at Morden Wharf, North Greenwich opened on the same day, coded MG. One of the routes in from New Cross (making room for the 1 and its WHVs) was the 129, taking with it WVLs 350-357 and

removing the variety seen when operated by its previous garage. The 188 was pencilled in for allocation from 11 November.

WHV 17 lost its Zoopla ad in May. In order to supply refurbished WVNs for the Wimbledon tennis service during June (this

year's winners being Roger Federer and Garbine Muguruza), twelve WVNs stored since their ejection from the 259 (and awaiting refurbishment for the 131) were returned to service at Northumberland Park. More surreally, WVN 32 was put into action at Peckham! In August additional stored WVNs were deployed to Merton to provide extras on the 77 (officially known as 777) during the extent of reconstruction of the railway lines into Waterloo. Further oddments into Merton included three 'Fugly' WHVs ex-Putney.

On 26 August the win of the 5 and 115 from Stagecoach East London enabled some spare WVLs to join 31 new EHs on an increasingly enormous River Road runout. Two days earlier, the announcement of the loss of the 474 for 2018 implementation would even that up in Stagecoach's favour just a little.

WVL 334 was the first 'X26' motor out of refurbishment during July, returning to Croydon in allover red and now single-doored with luggage racks and a new grey moquette designed to reduce the colour clash from acquired buses. WVL 343 emerged from Hants & Dorset Trim late in August and WVL 339 was September's output. At the same time, the 5's backup WVLs and the WVNs intended for the 131 were being treated. The spare stock of WVNs awaiting refurbishment saw continuous action, six serving with Green Street Green on extras on the 161.

Left: **Carnival weekend of 2017 saw the usual oddities as local services were augmented with whatever could be spared form a Sunday PVR. One such was WHV 7 (LJ61 GXE) of New Cross, coming across from the 436 to add muscle to the 36, which also featured buses from Stockwell. It is seen on Monday 28th August at Harrow Road, Prince of Wales.** *Author*

Left: **The other New Cross Carnival route was the 36X, operated with Es and WVLs. Heading in the opposite direction on 28 August is WVL 387 (LX11 CVM) of the 171's batch, with a red replacement bumper panel contrasting with its existing London Central livery.** *Author*

Left: **On 30 September 2017 the 131 was won by London General and put into Merton, but to make room there the 155 was pushed out to Stockwell with its WHVs. Seen at Tooting Broadway on the first day is WHV 84 (BD65 EVR).** *Author*

Right: **On its first day back with Merton in three decades, the 131 could be seen fielding four types. The main component was from the WVN class of former First Volvo B9TLs, one of which is WVN 28 (BG59 FXE) in Wimbledon Broadway on 30 September 2017.** *Author*

Right: **Three WVLs new to the 19 also featured on the first day of the 131 under London General; here at Kingston on the morning of 30 September is WVL 482 (LJ61 NWR).** *Author*

Right: **Quite unexpectedly, three WHVs turned out on the 131, whereas they more properly belonged on the 280. Calling at Kingston's Cromwell Road bus station on the morning of 30 September is WHV 21 (LJ61 NVG). Finally, the only non-Volvo out on that day was E 226!** *Author*

After thirty years, Merton returned to the 131 on 30 September with the route's takeover by London General. The majority of the new complement was WVNs, but five 61- and 12-reg WVLs came across from Stockwell. Inevitably, WHVs of both bodies counted themselves in within the first week, plus Es! To make room at Merton the 155 and its WHVs were transferred to Stockwell, allowing the buses to wander to the 118, itself recently shuffled around from Metrobus's Croydon (and prior to that, Merton itself). WVL 332 appeared on the 155 on 12 October, with home-made blinds (which were also widespread on the 131s at first, especially one hair-raising example which otherwise still showed blinds from River Road's school route 649, all the way across town!

Above: **The 22's conversion to hybrid was effectively completed in October 2017 with the delivery of MHV 86-99, disregarding the fact that there were already two other types at Putney. For a change carrying a London registration, MHV 95 (LF67 EWU) is seen at the end of Lower Richmond Road in Putney on 26 October.** *Author*

Right: **Naturally, Putney put its new MHVs out on the 14 and 74 as soon as they arrived, and here outside the Odeon on 26 October is MHV 92 (LF67 EWR).** *Author*

To accompany the retention of the 22 and thereby a clean sweep ensuring Putney's survival for at least five more years, fifteen more MHVs were ordered, despite the likelihood of the garage now operating three types. They began entering service on 12 October, naturally not only on the 22.

A concerted push by Google to market its new Pixel 2 phone saw thirty London buses commissioned with white and black all-over adverts in November, and Putney contributed WHVs 115-121. The difference was that now vehicle fronts were included, presenting a more easily recognisable image than ads ending only at the front.

11 November saw WHVs 168-196 enter service at Morden Wharf on the 188, picked up that day from Abellio. A couple of them were fitted with Camberwell blinds as they arrived and used there from 23 October to let

PVLs leave early. The 176 was also taken over by London Central, returning to Camberwell for the first time since 1990, but new EHs formed the majority and the only WHVs present were already based or transferred in. Existing MHVs soon appeared as well. Shortly after delivery WHVs 179 and 188 exchanged identities.

From 27 October until mid-November the 93 gained back its DOEs after their modification to Euro 6 emissions specification, letting the loaned MHVs return to Peckham; MHV 40 was the last to operate at Sutton, on 17 October.

In spite of the dominance of the Volvo B5LH in this particular generation of London buses, Go-Ahead cancelled an order for 22 that were intended to assume the 44 as part of the clean sweep of south-west London tenders in October; instead Wrights got the

nod to supply 22 new StreetDeck hybrids (WSDs).

Strange workings by the end of 2017 and into 2018 included Merton WHVs on the 164, Stockwell WHVs on the 432 and Morden Wharf WHVs on the 286.

Disposals of the B9TL variant of the WVL class began at the end of 2017, despite there being far older buses still in the fleet; first went Putney's WVL 496-508 off lease, followed by three ex-Bexleyheath examples.

WHVs 115-119 lost their Google Pixel adverts in January 2018. In February so did WHVs 120 and 121, but WHV 158 received an advert for Oyster Hopper and WHV 164 one for Isabel Marant.

On 17 March the 1 was reallocated once again, this time from New Cross to Morden Wharf. On the 31st the 188 was transferred from Morden Wharf to Camberwell, to fill the space from the loss of both the 68 and 468 on that day. Loosely associated from those

Above: **Still carrying Metrobus fleetnames when espied coming through New Cross on 2 April 2018 is WHV 44 (BP15 OLO), transferred to New Cross.** *Author*

Left: **WVL 275 (LX59 CYO) was an unusual sight on the 131 coming into Kingston on 5 April 2018; this originally New Cross bus found its way to River Road and thence to Merton; stablemate WVL 276 also landed at Merton and had just departed in the opposite direction.** *Author*

transfers was the appearance of two MHVs at Morden Wharf and two WHVs at Peckham, disrupting what order there was. Stragglers from the 59-reg batch of WVLs were already drifting to Morden Wharf and Merton for a bit of variety.

In March WHV 140 gained an ad for Michelin, joined in April by WHV 163, though WHV 164 lost its Isabel Marant ad. April also saw the completion of the X26's refurbishment programme with the outshopping of WVL 338, but the promised branding remained nowhere to be found.

The delivery of EHs for the 171 and their entry into service during May and June allowed the WVL 386-412 batch to stand

down for return off lease, despite their mere seven years of age.

For a long time there had been the promise of two all-electric Volvo B5LHCs with Wrightbus SRM bodywork, and after long delays actually inventing and manufacturing the vehicles' charging infastructure, the two appeared in June 2018 as VHP 1 and 2. Assigned to London Central, their intended allocation is to Peckham for the 37, with charging stations erected at Peckham bus station and at Putney Heath.

Above: **Absolut vodka's 2018 campaign combined LGBT rainbow themes with the LED advertising panel so that the message is beamed to the appropriate local inhabitants, as we see on this 23 June 2018 photo of Putney's WHV 118 (BV66 VHW) laying over at the traditional, but lately much expanded, Green Man stand at Putney Heath.** *Author*

Left: **Slowly but surely, the elegant and discreet London General livery of 2000 is disappearing from the capital. By the time this account was completed and submitted in August 2018, some of the B9TLs that carried it for Go-Ahead have been refurbished (with the accompanying all-red repaint) and others have been sold. WVL 382 (LX60 DXP), now based at Stockwell and nominally allocated to the 432, is seen taking the livery through Parliament Square on 1 July 2018. The 87 is scheduled for EHs, but tends to be second-rung enough at Stockwell to accept all the flotsam picked up by that garage from one location or another.** *Author*

Registrations

VE 1-3	LX58 CWK-M
WVL 274-302	LX59 CYL/O/P/S-W/Y/Z, CZA-D/F-H/J-P/R-V
WVL 303-333	LX59 CYA/C-H/J/K, CZW/Y/Z, DAA/O/U, DBO/U/V/Y/Z, LX59 DCE/F/O/U/V/Y/Z, DDA/E/F/J/K
WVL 334-349	LX59 DDL/N/O/U/V/Y/Z, DEU, DFA/C-G/J/K
WVL 350-385	LX60 DVY/Z, DWA/C-G/J-P/U-W/Y/Z, DXA-H/J/K/M/O/P/R-T
WVL 386-421	LX11 CVL-P/R-W/Y/Z, CWA/C-E/G/J-P/R/T-W/Y/Z, CXA-D
WVL 422-434	LX11 FHV/W-Z, FJA/C-F/J/K/N/O
WVL 435-456	LJ61 GWU-Z, GXA-D, GWD-G/K-P, GVP, GVT
WVL 457-495	LJ61 NUM/O/P/U-Y, NVA/B, NWW/X, LJ12 CHC, LJ61 NWZ, NXA-F, LJ61 NWM-O, LJ12 CHD, LJ61 NWR, LJ12 CHF/G, LJ61 NWU/V/Z, LJ61 NWA-H
WVL 496-508	LJ62 KXX/Z, KYA/G, KOX, KZD/P, KBY, KCU, KDV/Z, KLC/S
WHV 1-16	LJ61 GVW-Z, GWA/C, GXE-H/K-P
WHV 17-31	LJ61 NVC-H/K-N, LJ12 CHH, LJ61 NWR, LJ12 CHF/G
WHV 32-41	LJ62 KFD/F/U, KGF/G/N/Y, KHF/V, KKP
WHV 42-80	BP15 OLN/M/O/V/U/R/T/W/X, OMA, BF65 WJA, BP15 OMC/E/B/K/J/L/F/D, BF65 WJD/E/C/K/N/M/J/V, BF65 WJU/O/G/X, BF65 WKA, WJY, WKB, WJZ, WKG/D/C/E
WHV 81-110	BD65 EVN, BF65 WLH, BD65 EVM/R/P/T/U/X/Y/W, BD65 EWA/P/O/S/Y/Z, BT65 JGF, BD65 EWV, BT65 JGU, BD65 EWX, EVV, EWN/R/U, BT65 JFZ, JGO, BD65 EWW, BT65 JGV, BD65 EXA, EWT
WHV 112-167	BV66 VHN-P/R/T/U/W-Z, VJN-P/U/Y/Z, VKB, VLE/M/K/F/H, ZRZ, BV66 VHJ/K/P/A, VHH, ZRY, BT66 MSO/U, BV66 VJA/C-G/J-M, BV66 VKA/C/D/J/L/N/G/VHL, BV66 ZSD, BT66 MSV/X, MPU, MSY, BV66 VLO/R
WHV 168-196	LF67 EXA-E/G/H/J-P/R-Z, EYA-D/G/H/J
EHV 1-16	BK15 AZR/T, BJ15 TWL, BL15 HBK, BL15 TWP, BL15 HBJ/O/P/U/X-Z, BL15 HCA/C/D, HBN
MHV 1-20	BU16 OYJ/M/L/K/N-P/R-T/V-Z, OZA/E/C/D/B
MHV 21-55	BV66 VKN-P, BG66 MHX, BV66 VKR-U, BG66 MHY, BV66 VKW, BG66 MHZ, BV66 VKX/Z, BG66 MKA/C/D, BV66 VHG, BG66 MJE/F/J/O, BV66 VHA, BG66 MJU/V, BV66 VHC/D, BG66 MJX/Y, BV66 VGU/X-Z/ BT66 MPE/F/O
MHV 56-85	BV66 VKG/H/J/K, VFT, VHE, VKL, VFU/W-Z, VGA/C-G/J-P, BG66 MHV, BV66 VKM/C/D/P
MHV 86-99	LF67 EWK-P/R-Y
VHP 1, 2	BV18 YAD/E
VM 1	BJ11 XJG
V 6	BF63 HFE
V 6 (ii)	BJ14 KTL

Date	Deliveries	Licensed for Service
10.08	VE 1-3	VE 1-3 (**AF**)
10.09	WVL 274-285	
11.09	WVL 286, 288, 289, 292, 294-296, 298, 301-303, 311, 312, 317-325, 327	WVL 274-298, 300-302 (**NX**)
12.09	WVL 304-308, 310, 326, 328-333	WVL 303-308, 310-333 (**PM**)
01.10	WVL 299, 309, 334-344	WVL 299 (**NX**), WVL 309 (**PM**)
02.10	WVL 345-349	WVL 334-349 (**BE**)
12.10	WVL 350-356, 359	
01.11	WVL 357, 358, 360-385	WVL 350-357, 360, 362, 363, 375-379 (**BX**)
02.11		WVL 358, 359, 361, 364-374, 380-385 (**BX**)
03.11	WVL 386-412	
04.11	WVL 413-421	WVL 386-412 (**NX**), 413-421 (**SI**)
05.11	VM 1	VM 1 (**SI**)

08.11	WVL 422-434	WVL 422-434 (**SI**)
09.11	WVL 435-452, WHV 1, 2	WVL 435-452 (**Q**)
10.11	WVL 453, 454, WHV 3-14, 16	WVL 453, 454 (**Q**), WHV 3-14, 16 (**Q**)
11.11	WHV 15	WHV 15 (**Q**)
12.11	WVL 455, 456	WVL 455, 456 (**BX**)
02.11	WVL 457-468, 470-480, 482, 485-495	
	WHV 17-26, 28-30, 32	
03.11	WVL 469, 481, 483, 484	WVL 457-467 (**BE**), 468-480 (**AL**), 481-495 (**SW**)
	WHV 27, 31	WHV 17-31 (**SW**)
10.11	WVL 496-508, WHV 32-41	WVL 496-507 (**AF**), WHV 32-41 (**AF**)
11.11		WVL 508 (**AF**), WHV 41 (**AF**),
10.13	V 6	V 6 (**Q**)
08.14	V 6 (ii)	V 6 (ii) (**Q**)
08.15	WHV 42-51	WHV 42-51 (**C**)
09.15	WHV 52-68	WHV 52-68 (**C**)
10.15	WHV 69-80	WHV 69-80 (**C**)
11.15	WHV 81-83, 85, 86, 88, 90	
12.15	WHV 84, 87, 89, 91, 92, 94-97,	WHV 82-92, 94-96, 99-101, 104 (**AL**)
	99-102, 104-109	
01.16	WHV 93, 98, 103, 110	WHV 81, 93, 97, 98, 102, 103 (**AL**),
		WHV 105-110 (**A**)
09.16	MHV 56-60, 62-73, 83-85	MHV 56-60, 62-73, 83-85 (**Q**)
10.16	MHV 22, 23, 25-28, 40, 41, 61, 74-82	MHV 23, 25, 27, 28, 41 (**PM**)
	WHV 112-127, 129-133, 143-145,	WHV 112, 114 (**AF**),
	147, 150, 152, 153, 156-158	WHV 143-145, 147, 150, 152, 153, 156 (**MW**)
11.16	MHV 21, 24, 29-36, 38, 39, 42-46, 81	MHV 21, 22, 24, 26, 29-31, 33-36, 39, 45, 46 (**PM**)
	WHV 128, 134, 146, 148, 149, 151,	MHV 81 (**Q**)
	154, 155	WHV 146, 148, 149, 151, 154, 155, 157 (**MW**)
		WHV 113, 115-134, 158 (**AF**)
12.16	WHV 135-142, 159-167	MHV 32, 37, 38, 42, 43, 47, 48, 50-55 (**PM**)
		MHV 61 (**Q**), WHV 135, 141, 161 (**AF**)
01.17		MHV 44 (**PM**), MHV 49 (**Q**),
		WHV 137, 139, 140, 159, 162-164, 166 (**AF**)
02.17		WHV 136, 138, 142, 160, 165, 167 (**AF**)
10.17	WHV 168-196, MHV 86-99	MHV 86-99 (**AF**), WHV 168, 172 (**Q**)
11.17		WHV 177, 178, 183 (**Q**)
		WHV 169-171, 173-176, 179-182, 184-196 (**MG**)

Acquired from First London, 31.03.12
WVN 1-53   ex-First London VN 37804-37813, 37816, 37819, 37814, 37815, 37817, 37818,
              37820-37841, 37843, 37845, 37846, 37848, 37856-37858, 37944-37951)

Acquired from Volvo, 01.09.15
WVL 509, 510 Volvo B5TL/Wrightbus Gemini 3 H41/21D,
              ex-Arriva VGD 1 and Metroline VW 1469)

Acquired from Volvo, 04.16
BX14 TJV   Volvo B5TL/Wrightbus Gemini 3 H41/21D,
              into stock 06.16 as **WHV 111**)

Disposals
08.13	VM 1
03.14	V 6
04.15	V 6 (ii)
11.17	WVL 496-508
02.18	WVL 369, 372, 377
03.18	WVL 370, 371
05.18	WVL 373, 374, 389, 394, 400-406

Sovereign

VH 1-23, VHR 45203-45208

Descending from the old BTS and Sovereign operators, London Sovereign by 2012 had been severed from London United and now fell under Veolia Transdev. Its main route, operated from Edgware (BT) was the trunk route 13, which since OPO conversion on 22 October 2005 had operated SLE-class Scanias, accompanied from later in the decade by all-Polish SPs. In December 2012 its retention by Sovereign was announced and an order for 23 Wrightbus Gemini 2-bodied Volvo B5LHs was placed to furnish a PVR of 21 in time for a start date of 31 August 2013.

Later in 2013 the company's 292 was also retained, ensuring the future of the existing SLEs in the short term.

On 2 July VH 2 was delivered, followed on the 4th by VH 1 and two more shortly afterwards. Weighing in at 11,881kg unlade, they seated 60 (H39/21D) and externally, sported a new Transdev logo all in lower case. Entry into service commenced on 10 August with ten VHs, and the rest were put into service on the 31st in time for the contract start, which also encompassed the N13. Just VH 23 was a latecomer, but the fleet was complete by September.

Little ensued thereafter, other than wanderings to newly commissioned school route 605 from October. However, at the end of March 2014 RATP Dev reached out and purchased Sovereign from its neighbour, reuniting it once again with London United.

Below: **Showing the shortlived revised Transdev logo at Charing Cross on 24 February 2014 is Edgware's VH 6 (BD13 OHZ).** *Author*

The transfer took effect from 29 April, and obviously that was the end of the new logo barely as soon as it had started; after a five-month lull, a new London Sovereign logo was worked up, to RATP's house style with the river Seine running though.

Between February and May 2014 VH 14 carried an all-over ad for Karen Millen. VH visits to the 183 commenced on 12 May and soon spread to the 114, mostly working off the 605 school bus; finally the 292 completed the set of routes seen by VHs. A PVR hike to the 13 at the beginning of 2015 necessitated the increased appearance of VLEs, SLEs and SPs, but the route was actually lucky to dodge withdrawal in its entirety when an extremely ill-advised consultation that would have subsumed its role into the 113, 139 and 189, and thereby transferred its contract to an extended 139, was slammed in the press and subsequently rejected.

In February 2015 another Karen Millen ad was commissioned; this time it was applied to VH 13 and lasted six months. After that, VH 21 took on an ad for GANT between September and December and VH 1 served as Sovereign's Poppy Bus.

Probably the greatest achievement of the Sovereign VHs has been in their prompting of new parent London United to place repeat orders for the type, and over a hundred were in service by the end of 2016.

Top: **VH 14 (BT13 YWN) spent much of 2014 with an all-over ad for Karen Millen, and on 1 April is seen carrying it out of Golders Green.** *Author*

Above: **Just a rear ad on VH 13 (BT13 YWL), seen inside the bus station at Golders Green on 28 August 2014.** *Author*

Left: **London Sovereign's new logo is captured in its full glory as VH 2 (BD13 OHV) crosses Trafalgar Square on the morning of 10 September 2015.** *Author*

The prototype, carrying registration LJ16 EXD but not to be licensed with that mark, posed at Covent Garden on 16 March for the London Transport Museum but returned to Wrights at Ballymena straight after. Its capacity was H45/21D and length was 10.6m. The intent was to use them on the 13 so as to be able to cascade six VHs to the 183 and fulfil its upcoming contract requirements. VHR 45203 was taken into stock in June, now registered LJ16 MUV; the rest would be 66-reg. Pending their arrival, some of the incoming VH batch from associate London United were diverted to Edgware, due to a remarkable lack of foresight on the part of the company's planners in thinking that Hammersmith Bridge would be anywhere near ready for double-deckers to return to the 72, but ordering them anyway! On 18 July the new VHs began appearing on not only the 13, but the 114 and 183. Even then, the complement that came in was quickly rotated out and replaced by earlier examples, due to the nearside blind boxes being in a different position at either end of the batch and this being felt unduly important.

There was, however, another B5LH variant still to come, and this was rather more spectacular in that it carried Wrightbus's new SRM body, which was otherwise the Borismaster's body adapted for the B5LH, with one staircase and an asymmetric rear, although the burgundy interior of the LT was retained. London Sovereign ordered six, as the body was available to anyone, and tacked them onto the end of the VH class as VHR 45203-45208.

The 114 was lost to Metroline on 3 September and the 183 gained a complement of VHs as intended.

VHR 45203 moved to Edgware in September for training and on 19 October entered service, but rather than the prestige 13, it was entrusted to humble school route 618. After an afternoon on similar route 605 and thence to the 292, its first try at the 13 was on 2 November and it stayed thereon thereafter. The H14's schoolday double deck working was entrusted to VHs from the new batch from late November.

VH 17 was the company's 2016 representative in Poppy Bus livery in November, but the scheme was actually exactly the same as the previous year's.

Finally for 2016, all five remaining 'Fakemasters' entered service on the 13, VHR 45208 on 2 December, VHR 45204 the day after, VHR 45205 on the 9th and the other two on 9 January 2017.

However, the 13 passed to Tower Transit on 1 April 2017 as part of a convoluted and most underhand second try at hacking buses out of Oxford Street; in this case it assumed the 82's roads to Victoria. Some compensation, but not for the capacity lost along the Finchley Road, saw the 139 extended from West Hampstead to Golders Green and its contract transferred to Sovereign, thus retaining use of the VHs and VHRs.

Left: **Outwardly identical to the Borismaster until you get to behind the staircase, the Wrightbus SRM-bodied Volvo B5LH formed the VHR class with Sovereign, and VHR 45203 (LJ16 MUV), seen at Golders Green on a gloomy 23 January 2017, was the first.** *Author*

Left: **The 13 as it stood was on its way out anyway, but allegedly due to the confusion experienced by passengers attempting to board a VHR as if it were a Borismaster, all six were switched to the 183. Here at Golders Green's other end on 3 April is VHR 45204 (LJ66 EZO).** *Author*

Right: **The 13 effectively ceded its role to the 139, in order to reduce traffic along the Finchley Road. On 3 April at the revamped Oxford Circus VH 19 (BT13 YWR) illustrates the new order of Sovereign B5LHs in place of Metroline VPs.** *Author*

Right: **The handful of Gemini 3-bodied VHs also made the move fron 13 to 139, and at the Waterloo turning lane on 3 April 2017 we see VH 45160 (LJ65 FZS).** *Author*

Right: **Naturally, the six Fakemasters soon joined in on the recast 139, 3 April seeing VHR 45208 (LJ66 EZU) leaving Golders Green.** *Author*

A new advert for 2017 was for the upcoming 2018 Winter Olympics to be held in South Korea; VH 2 (or 45102) was treated in April 2017 and lasted until June.

The takeover of the 142 on 6 January 2018 was accomplished with ADE-class E40Ds transferred from associated London United, but the first day saw three VHs from Edgware and this type continued appearing. The 183's VHRs were transferred from Edgware to Harrow with the rest of that route on that day.

Registrations

VH 1-23	BD13 OHU/V-Z, OJA-E, OHJ, BT13 YWK/L/N/J/M/P/O/R/S/W/U/V
VHR 45203-45208	LJ16 MUV, LJ66 EZO/P/R/T/U

VHs 1-23 renumbered VHs 45101-45123 over 2017.

Date	Deliveries	Licensed for Service
07.13	VH 1-4	
08.13	VH 5-22	VH 1-22 (**BT**)
08.13	VH 23	VH 23 (**BT**)
06.16	VHR 45203	
10.16	VHR 45204-45208	
12.16		VHR 45204, 45205, 45208 (**BT**)
01.17		VHR 45206, 45207 (**BT**)

* VHs delivered in summer 2016 and transferred are covered in London United's chapter.

London United

VM and VH classes

Since low-floor double-deckers came along, London United had divided its affections fairly equally between Dennis and Volvo before being seduced completely by Scanias. As the Polish option fell away after 2011, a new generation of low-floors began to hit the streets; London United dabbled in Enviro400s, taking small batches of diesels and hybrids alike, but it was not until London Sovereign was brought back under common ownership with London United that Volvo chassis was looked at more seriously.

An MCV-bodied Volvo B9TL had been taken on loan from 18 October 2012; with a seating capacity of H41/22D and registered BF62 UXU, it was numbered VM 1 (at the same time as Docklands Buses was operating another demonstrator of that number!). Substantial weight savings had been achieved since the 'other' VM 1 of eighteen months senior. After a period in store and a trip back to Volvo for modifications, it was put into service at Hounslow on the H32 on 12 December, lasting until 25 July 2014, after which it was returned to Volvo and

Below: **VM 1 (BF62 UXU) spent eighteen months with London United, sharing the H32 with Scanias. On 29 April 2013 it is heading south along Convent Way in Southall.** *Terry Wong Min*

Left: **The Gemini 3 was already something of a comedown from its two predecessors, what with its mismatched upper- and lower-deck windows and glass where it didn't belong, but London United compounded all that by not having the headlights picked out in black. VH 36 (LJ15 JZN) entered service at Hounslow Heath on 4 June and is seen in Wood Street, Kingston.** *Author*

subsequently took up service with Wessex Connect.

At the end of 2014 London United was awarded a renewed contract for its existing 285, but with a long-awaited boost to double-deck operation. The resulting order for 28 Volvo B5LHs with Wrightbus's recently-revised Gemini 3 bodywork would also take in the forthcoming retention and similar restoration to double-deck of the 116, both routes being operated by Hounslow Heath garage. They would follow on from the VH class introduced by Sovereign and represent the increasing coming together of the two companies. The purchase policy of the junior partner had influenced the senior!

Below: **VH 40 (LJ15 JZT) is seen on 4 July a little way down from the last picture, making the swing across what before 1990 used to be a through street.** *Author*

VHs 24-43 began arriving as early as April; VH 29 via the Belfast Bus Rally on the 25th of that month before boarding the boat. The new buses were stored at the former NCP/NSL garage at Twickenham before being readied for service. The 285's contract commenced on 27 June but eight entered service on the 4th, with three more turning out on the H91. This was only a one-off, however, due to the need to fill in for the 285's regular DEs being needed to take blind veterans to an event at Buckingham Palace, and proper squadron entry was implemented on 13 June, closer to the date. Most of the DEs were earmarked for transfer to Sovereign to take up the 326, with the shortfall propping up numbers elsewhere.

A one-bus increase to the 285 between its award and implementation saw the order increased by one to 29, and July saw the delivery of VHs 44-51, the 116's intended buses. These were all in service by 25 August, four days before the contract date. Inevitably the batches became mixed, and Hounslow Heath would also put them out on the H91 from time to time.

The VH class was set to grow when London United's bid to keep the 72 but with double-deckers was accepted at the end of 2015. The company also won back the 85 and kept hold of the 65, the latter with a 'new buses' element. Accordingly, in December 47 new VHs were ordered, but now with the controversial new Gemini 3 bodywork. The order was increased to 56 when it was realised that the current drive towards 100% hybrid buses in central London rendered the 94's remaining TLAs unwelcome; accordingly, the first eight of the VH order were put into service on the 94 as soon as they arrived, 10 March 2016 being their first day. Fourteen were in service by April.

There was an important change at this point, and a most unfortunate one; London United had invested in a new computerised fleet management system of the same type that had made a mess of First London's fleet numbering a decade previously, and the new buses inexplicably had forty-five thousand, one hundred added to their class codes.

Sixteen of the new VHs (45167-45182) were earmarked for the 85, scheduled to be taken over from London General. Tolworth was the operating garage, and it prepared for its new task by putting some of them into service early, on the 131 and school route 662, from 27 May. The 85 was duly assumed on 2 July, filling in nicely for the concurrent loss of the

Above: **Four of the new VHs went into Fulwell to fulfil contractual requirements that demanded a new bus component on the 65, otherwise retained with its existing 09-reg Scanias. On 19 July 2016 VH 45184 (LJ16 EWF) is seen in Kingston, and almost not, no thanks to a parked car!** *Author*

57, and from time to time they would wander to the 71, transferred from Fulwell on this day to make up the shortfall. The 'new buses' component of the 65 was fulfilled with VHs 45183-45186 into Fulwell, though the first of these left soon after to top up Tolworth. And then there was the quandary of what to do with the remainder of the order, as someone in officialdom had jumped the gun quite

severely on the likelihood of Hammersmith Bridge to be able to accept double-deckers and thus ordered them anyway against the 72's upcoming new contract. This structure being no more likely to be repaired than at any point in the last quarter of a century, which had obliged demotion of all the routes crossing it to single-deck operation in the first place, London United had to rethink, and it

Right: **The summer switch of VHs between Shepherd's Bush and Edgware brought VH 45197 (LJ16 EWW) to the former, though not with any change to the London Sovereign fleetnames it was already carrying. It is heading round Marble Arch on 14 August.** *Author*

was decided to send some to Sovereign for the 13. That company's travails with its new VHs are covered in the preceding chapter, but almost as soon as the new VHs were in place at Edgware they were exchanged for newer examples coming off the production line. The rationale was that the side blind boxes were in different positions between VHs 45153-45182 (lower) and the rest (higher), although the 13 and 94 shared much of the same ground once in town.

In August five more VHs were ordered, but these were substantially different to the run-of-the-mill service buses. As the Kingston University contracts had been gained from Rotala, something special was called for and the company, under the guise of its new private-hire arm United Transit, went all-out. VHs 45209-45215 (their stock numbers skipping the six Wrightbus SRM-bodied Volvo B5LHs for Sovereign) were specified to the 11.4m length (H49/28D) with exposed staircase glass, wood-effect flooring and WiFi. Until they arrived, VHs 45162-45166 brought back from their brief spell at Edgware, plus new VHs 45201 and 45202, stood in for them on the KU-routes once the university term began late in September. All were gussied up for the occasion through the application of a vinyl front in the grey colours of Kingston University, and the operation was run from Twickenham, the former NCP Challenger garage. Completing the original order, VH

45200 was added to Shepherd's Bush for the 94.

Four of the six *bona fide* Kingston University VHs arrived in October and entered service on 7 November, allowing VHs 45162-45166 to return to normal service (VH 45162 at Tolworth and the other three at Fulwell), but the newer pair remained until VHs 45214 and 45215 arrived in April 2017.

Very, very slowly, Hounslow Heath's VHs started having their new fleetnumbers applied, the first examples appearing as such in February 2017.

The win of the 18 from Metroline West was London United's coup of 2017, and in May 36 VHs were ordered, with the intent that several more existing examples would be redeployed to Park Royal to join them when the route was assumed.

A Dart and Enviro200 shortage at Fulwell during the spring led to the effective double-decking of the 216, with the garage's VHs playing their part.

On 16 October the Kingston University VHs were transferred from Twickenham to Hounslow Heath. The thirty-eight VHs for the 18 from 11 November comprised VHs 45216-45251, this time taking the Birmingham registrations of their dealership when London United had hitherto been one of the only firms to keep registering their vehicles in London (and at the time when Go-Ahead now resumed London registrations on its concurrent batch of WHVs!). The former Tower Transit Atlas Road garage was taken on lease by RATP to allow Park Royal to close, but confusingly the Park Royal name would migrate across with it, albeit now with the

code RP. The rest of the 18's requirement was made up of twelve VHs leaving Sovereign, replaced there by reactivated Scanias (SPs).

Three more B5LHs (VH 45255-45257) were ordered in October against the award of school route 635. In October VH 45103 received an ad plugging Taylor Swift's new album, 'Reputation', and November saw VH 45121 receive one for Too Faced. Both lasted until January 2018.

VHs 45209-45215 were transferred to Tolworth with the Kingston University services in time for the beginning of the 2018 spring term. In January 2018 VHs 45255-45257 were delivered, but would be regular Hounslow Heath buses rather than dedicated route 635 motors as planned. In contravention of that contractual obligation, two of them promptly transferred to Edgware!

The award of the 105 prompted an order for sixteen more VHs, but those would be the last B5LHs for the moment as the Enviro400 was beginning to catch the company's eye again, and indeed a 2018 order for four ADEs snarled the orderly numbering system that had been predicated on vehicle blocks. VHs 45262-45277 entered service with the 105's new London United contract applying from 30 June, operating out of Hounslow Heath.

Left: **Cuts to other London United and Sovereign PVRs helped release a handful of VHs to support 36 new examples entering service on 11 November 2017. Seen at Euston, VH 45185 (LJ16 EWG) came from Fulwell, where it had been one of the new-vehicle component delivered for the latest London United contract on the 65.** *Author*

Below: **VH 45216 (BF67 GKD) was one of the 36 new Volvo B5LHs for the 18, seen crossing Warren Street on the first afternoon with its RP garage code clearly displayed (though, unfortunately, no running number to go with it).** *Author*

Above: **On 30 June 2018 the 105 was taken over by London United, which added it to Hounslow Heath's roster. Entering service on that day were sixteen new VHs, of which VH 45276 (LF18 AXU) is seen passing Southall station.** *Author*

Right: **Nine months after entering service on the 18, VH 45241 (BF67 GMV) has had a little alteration done to the blind box; unfortunately, modern accessibility statutes don't permit blinds to be put in there that have any information on them other than the bare minimum. It is seen crossing the Euston Road's junction with Baker Street on 1 July 2018.** *Author*

Registrations

VM 1	BF62 UXU
VH 24-43	LJ15 JYY/Z, JZA/C-H/K-P/R/T-W
VH 44-52	LJ15 LAA/E/O, LBA/E-G/K/L
VH 45153-45161	LJ65 FZK-P/R-T
VH 45162-45199	LJ65 FZU*, LJ16 EVD/F-H/K-N/P/R/T-Y/EWA-H/K-P/R/T-Z
VH 45200-45202	LJ66 TRZ, TSO/U
VH 45209-45215	LJ66 TZL, DZS, TZW, TZM, TZN, LJ17 WUK, WUL
VH 45216-45251	BF67 GKD/E/G/J/K/X/Y, GLZ, GMO/Y, GKL/O/N/P/U/V, GLK, GKZ, GLJ/V/Y, GMG/E/U/X/V/Z, GNK/J/N/U/O/X/V, GUD, GNP
VH 45255-45257	LC67 ADU/X/V
VH 45262-25277	LF18 AXB/C/H/D/M/N/K, AWO, AXJ/A/R/S/O/P/U/T

VH 45162 re-registered LJ16 KLV after entering service.
VHs 24-52 renumbered VHs 45124-45152 over 2017.

Date	Deliveries	Licensed for Service
10.12	VM 1	
12.12		VM 1 (**AV**)
04.15	VH 24, 25, 27, 28, 31, 36-40	
05.15	VH 26, 29, 30, 32-35, 41, 42	
06.15	VH 43	VH 24-43 (**HH**)
07.15	VH 44, 45, 48, 51	
08.15	VH 46, 47, 49, 50, 52	VH 44-52 (**HH**)
02.16	VH 45153-45161	
03.16		VH 45153-45161 (**S**)
04.16	VH 45162-45174	VH 45162-45166 (**S**)
05.16	VH 45175-45182	VH 45167, 45168 (**TV**)
06.16	VH 45183-45199	VH 45169-45182 (**TV**)
07.16		VH 45183-45186 (**FW**)
		VH 45187, 45188, 45189, 45194, 45197 (**BT**)
08.16		VH 45190-45193, 45195, 45196, 45198, 45199 (**S**)
09.16	VH 45200-45202	VH 45201, 45202 (**NC**)
10.16	VH 45209-45213	
11.16		VH 45209-45213 (**NC**)
04.17	VH 45214, 45215	VH 45215 (**NC**)
07.17		VH 45214 (**NC**)
10.17	VH 45216-45219, 45221, 45222, 45226-25231, 45233-45236, 45238, 45240, 45243	
11.17	VH 45220, 45223-45225, 45232, 45237, 45239, 45241, 45242, 45244-45251	VH 45216-45251 (**RP**)
01.18	VH 45255-45257	
02.18		VH 45255-45257 (**HH**)
05.18	VH 45262-45265	
06.18	VH 45266-45277	

Disposals
07.13	VM 1

First London

VN 37773-37984, 37988-37996, 36101-36165, 36291-36295

First London was an early adopter of the Volvo B9TL; both Capital and Centrewest ends had alternated B7TL deliveries with those of Dennis Tridents, but the B9TL would become more numerous here than the Enviro400.

The ball was set rolling when the contract for the 83, already incumbent with Alperton, was awarded in February 2009 and an order placed in June for 31 B9TLs with Wrightbus Gemini 2 bodywork. The contract applied from 12 September, furnishing a PVR of 28.

VN 37773, the first of the 83's batch, was ready by 21 June when it arrived at Volvo's Brimsdown facility for pre-service tests,

but the bulk of them didn't start appearing until September and then only to Volvo at Brimsdown before release to First. VN 37788 was displayed at Coach & Bus at the NEC on 7 and 8 October, but finally deliveries picked up and VN 37794 was put into service on 3 November. From the outset they wandered to the 79 and 92 and then to the 245.

As the VNs were entering service, very slowly, First placed another order, this time for sixty to furnish the tendering wins of the 259 and 476 (already operated by Northumberland Park with VNL-class (originally VTL-class) Volvo B7TLs) and the 58, operated by Lea Interchange. The initial

Below: **On 18 October 2010 Alperton's VN 37774 (LK59 CXM) sets off from Golders Green. The bonded windows give rather more gravitas, especially when they hide the mismatched height necessitated by the presence of the air chiller upstairs.**
Author

examples of these arrived in December, in advance of the 476's commencement date of 30 January. Northumberland Park's first batch comprised VNs 37804-37826 and VN 37811 was first into service on 3 February 2010. As well as their assigned 476, they soon made appearances on the 259 (prior to the delivery of its own batch) and the 67.

The order was then increased by 26 to reflect the 427's contract, retained by Hayes and due to replace the current TNLs. Hayes itself was used for storage of the incoming new buses.

First's preferred brand of seating, however, had come in for much criticism over its sheer lack of comfort, and on the VNs was replaced by Esteban Civic V2 seats in customary pairs not long after the 83's contingent had entered service. This was completed by March.

Following the loan for familiarisation purposes of Northumberland Park's VN 37815, Lea Interchange's first VN in service was VN 37827 on 4 March and all of VNs 37827-37843 were in place on the 58 by April. These differed by virtue of having Birmingham registrations rather than ones booked in north-west London, an unfortunate trend that would underscore the 'non-London' nature of these basically group-standard buses.

More VNs were on the cards when the 18's contract came up for renewal and the incumbent First won it on the basis of replacing its controversial artics with double-deckers, and rather more of them than previously. The order, placed in March for September fulfilment, comprised 53 VNs.

Top: **VN 37782 (LK59 CWY) departs through West Hendon on 30 April 2011, showing us the rear aspect of this particular VN class within First London.** *Author*

Above: **The 245 was making itself a clear contender for double-deck operation through appearances by Volvo B9TLs like VN 37799 (LK59 FCP) at Golders Green on 18 October 2010. It eventually happened, three years later.** *Author*

Left: **Northumberland Park took two batches of VNs for the 476 and 259, and soon enough all mixed in service. At the Angel on 18 October 2010 is VN 37853 (BV10 WWL), showing the switch to Birmingham registrations.** *Author*

Right: **Wanderings from the 259 and 476 to the 67 threw up appearances like that of VN 37821 (LK59 FDL) on 13 February 2011 at Wood Green.** *Author*

Now followed VNs 37843-37864 for the 259, whose contract applied from 27 March; they were mixed with the 476's buses and as well as the 67, now started turning out on the 191, 341, 357 and school route 699.

Hayes's new VN fleet for the 427 comprised VNs 37865-37889 and the registrations here were helplessly mixed, to reflect that the manufacturers registered them in chassis number order and the operator had to pick its own numbering system out of that, if it hadn't been judicious enough to allocate fleetnumbers in the same manner. They began arriving from Northern Ireland between the end of March and mid-April and were taken into stock in April. 29 April was their start date on the 427 and N207 and all were in service within a week.

Below: **The 427's conversion from VNL to VN soon followed, with VN 37874 (BK10 MFN), at Uxbridge on 7 May 2012, the tenth of the batch.** *Author*

Left: **On 13 February 2011 Willesden Junction's VN 37936 (BF60 UVH) at Euston exemplifies the conversion of the 18 from artic back to double-deck buses.** *Author*

VN 37889 arrived in May as a top-up for Northumberland Park, whilst VN 37847 from the 476's batch was delayed due to an engine seizure incurred on its initial delivery run. It arrived on 28 May and entered service on 16 June. A lone B9TL, numbered VN 37943 to follow on for the fleetnumbers booked for the 18's awaited batch, came through Heysham Docks on 11 July and turned up at Alperton shortly after; it was a testbed incorporating a handful of modifications to the AdBlue filler and featuring a dual battery system for easier engine starts. Overall weight was also lower compared to earlier models, always a critical consideration with regard to fuel economy.

On 16 October First lost the 341 to Arriva and on 13 November the 92 was transferred from Alperton to Greenford, eliminating the likelihood of VN appearances on either.

The 18's VNs arrived in good time over September and October, early enough for some of them to be put to use on rail jobs and covering the Tube strike of 3 November. But on 13 November they all went into service on the 18 out of Willesden Junction, banishing artics from another London route.

Left: **Also at Euston but on 8 October 2011, VN 37900 (BF60 UUL) loads up ready to go, if just as far west as Harlesden.** *Author*

Above: **Of the 65 VNs taken for the 25 in 2011, VNs 36101-36135 had ZF gearboxes and VNs 36136-36165 by Voith. Lea Interchange's VN 36108 (BJ11 DTO) was one of the former, and is seen on 3 July in Ilford.** *Author*

Although First had been tilting towards the Enviro400 in its orders, the Volvo B9TL still figured large and no more so than when the 25 was won back from Stagecoach East London for June 2011 takeup and an order for sixty-five VNs was placed to replace its Citaro bendy buses. A problem was foreseen, however, in that there would not quite be enough numbers in the current series after VN 37943 unless they wanted to drift into the next block of thousands, and the 38000s were currently occupied by miscellaneous double-deckers. Instead, it was decided to plunder the under-served series currently held by

Scanias and number them VN 36101-36165.

They were delivered between 31 March and May and held at Lea Interchange ready for the 25's assumption on 25 June, but nine were licensed early and were put into service on the garage's existing route 58, following this with visits to DLR and Underground replacement services as fit.

On the same day as the VNs' takeover of the 25, Lea Interchange also took up the 26 and 30 with their new DN-class Enviro400s, and from the outset each route's type would appear on the other, though they were by no means mixed. VNs even tried out the RV1.

Right: **VN 36124 (BJ11 DTU) happens through Ilford at the beginning of a long slog west to Oxford Circus on 25 March 2012.** *Author*

In July an order was placed for 41 more VNs, nominally against the current contract for the 295, which had actually been running with First since the previous autumn. As decisions fluctuated between whether and how many of each of Volvos and Enviro400s (both diesel and hybrid) to buy, the VN order was revised by October so that most of them would take up the 23 on a temporary basis; eight others were earmarked for Northumberland Park and the 357, the retention of which was announced in July.

On 17 September a cross-link introduced from school route 616 to Lea Interchange's 58 brought a regular Northumberland Park VN onto the latter.

London's last articulated buses bowed out after 9 December with the conversion to SN-class Scania of the 207, but from the next day Hayes's VNs from the 427 could now make appearances and did so. Willesden Junction similarly let the odd VN out on the 487.

The 23's stopgap VNs started entering service at Westbourne Park on 10 January 2012, but this route was intended for a mix of DNs and DNHs in due course and a proportion of its VNs (plus five more new) would move over to the 266, which was to be taken up from Metroline on 19 May. The other eight would then be joined on the 295 by nine more new ones to be delivered by September. The 23's incoming batch were already making forays to the 295 as soon as they were put into service, and in January the semi-experimental VN 37943 found itself transferred from Hayes to Westbourne Park.

Top: **Put into service on the 23, VN 37953 (BN61 MXB) is seen at that route's Ladbroke Grove end on 17 June 2012.** *Author*

Above: **The same bus is caught at Paddington two months earlier, on 18 April.** *Author*

Left: **VN 37949 (BL61 ADO), seen at Walthamstow Central on 8 March 2012, didn't have long under that handle before Northumberland Park was sold to Go-Ahead and it was rechristened WVN 51.** *Author*

Right: **3 September 2011 sees Northumberland Park's VN 37853 (BV10 WWL) between Newington Green and Essex Road. This bus was transferred to Lea Interchange before the sale of Northumberland Park and woud thus stay with the fleet for a little longer.** *Author*

At the end of January followed VNs 37944-37952 for the 357; it will be noted that First resumed the series in the thirty-seven thousands.

Westbourne Park's VNs 37978 and 37979 were loaned to Hayes in February and used on the 427, albeit without blinds. Between 14 and 24 February the 357 was converted to VN operation at Northumberland Park, and unusually this batch tended to stay put. Regular strange visits from this garage continued to the 191 and now took in the 231. But a major change was in the offing when

First, financially troubled for a long time, announced on 29 February that it was going to sell Northumberland Park and its buses to Go-Ahead. The sale was signed on 19 March and completed on the 31st. A shuffle prior to the sale took VN 37889 to Alperton and VNs 37827-37841 from Lea Interchange were exchanged with Northumberland Park's VNs 37844, 37847, 37849-37855 and 37859-37864.

Out of the fleet, therefore, went VNs 37804-37841, 37843, 37845, 37846, 37848, 37856-37858 and 37944-37951, 53 of the 130 buses sold overall.

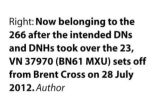

Right: **Now belonging to the 266 after the intended DNs and DNHs took over the 23, VN 37970 (BN61 MXU) sets off from Brent Cross on 28 July 2012.** *Author*

Right: **VN 36291 (BX12 CVO) was the first of five extras bought for the 266 and is seen on 28 July 2012 pulling onto one of the cramped stands at Brent Cross.** *Author*

February 2012 saw the first VN treated to an all-over advert livery, or at least three-quarters of it as the front was left in red. This was VN 37966, selling holidays in Bermuda.

In just about enough time to release the 266's intended VNs, the 23 was partially converted to DNH operation from 4 May. The 266's five top-ups were numbered VNs 36291-36295, dipping into the lower-numbered block again, and they began to arrive at Heysham Docks in the first week of May. They duly entered service on the 266 on the 19th alongside VNs 37953-37984 transferred, and in Atlas Road represented a new garage for the type.

In May VN 37952 received an ad for Thailand tourism, blue on the offside and black on the nearside, but in June the genre positively exploded, when, with the Olympics in mind, ten of Lea Interchange's route 25 VNs were liveried. West End musicals were the theme for VN 36138 (Jersey Boys), 36139 (Shrek) and 36155 (Billy Elliot), while seven, VNs 36107, 36124, 36141, 36144, 36147, 36149 and 36150, were treated to a scheme for the Samsung Galaxy 3 phone.

The Olympics proved an enormous success and brought regeneration to a long-neglected swathe of east London. For the duration, the 25's PVR was hiked by six, the VNs supplied by using otherwise stored outgoing TNs on the 58. There was also a temporary coversion of the 308 to double-deck, VNWs forming the basis but VNs occasionally appearing. June saw ten VNs given an ad for Visa, comprising VNs 36102, 36115, 36126, 37891, 37892, 37942, 37956, 37970 and 37975, although VN 37952 lost its Thailand ad and two more, VNs 36142 and 37955 gained one for Turkey.

Above right: **Seven Lea Interchange VNs based on the 25 were treated during the occasion of the Olympics to all-over ads for Samsung Galaxy phones; here at Stratford on 11 August is VN 36144 (BJ11 EAX).** *Author*

Right: **The 308 was outgrowing the Dart-sized buses based on it, and for the duration of the Olympics was converted to double-deck using some spare VNWs backed up by existing Lea Interchange VNs. Coming through Stratford on 4 August is VN 37860 (BV10 WWB).** *Author*

In August VN 37966 reverted to red (ex-Bermuda) as did two Visas (VNs 36102 and 36126). From mid-September a six-month swap of ten VNs was undertaken to compare their batches' engine fan performances; Willesden Junction sent VNs 37910, 37913, 37915, 37916 and 37942 to Atlas Road, gaining VNs 37964 and 37968-37971 in exchange.

October saw all the 'theatre' VNs lose their ad liveries plus all the Visas and four of the Samsungs; instead a new scheme for Apple bowed, with VNs 36115, 36116, 37799, 37920 and 37952-37954 treated in November. This was only for a month, however.

5 November saw a double-decker added to Alperton's 245 and VN 37889 brought in from Willesden Junction to furnish it.

First settled into a seeming torpor as 2012 rolled into 2013; the VN swaps ceased on 30 March and the quintets returned to their respective garages, but, as Northumberland Park garage had departed, so would follow the entire company. On 9 April the group announced its intention to sell, dividing the holding into two parts. Metroline would pick up the operations and buses of Alperton, Greenford, Hayes, Uxbridge and Willesden Junction, whilst Westbourne Park, Lea Interchange and Atlas Road would become Tower Transit under Australian ownership. 22 June was the takeover date; for the purposes of this book, 109 VNs passed to Metroline (being folded into its existing VW class) and 129 went to Tower Transit, and that was the end of First London.

Following the Olympics, the normal order of business resumed. The 23's remaining allocation arrived in August and September, these being twelve DNs intended to cascade the remaining twelve VNs to the 295. Skipping three numbers to reflect the delivery of three Green Line-spec Volvo B9TLs for First Berkshire (covered on page 178), VNs 37988-37996 entered service from 19 September onwards. Occasionally they turned out on the 28.

Registrations

VN 37773-37803	LK59 CWN-P/R/T-Z, CXA-H/L-P/U/V/X/Y
VN 37804-37826	LK59 FEP/T/U, FDV/X-Z, FEF-H/J/M/O, FDE-G/J
VN 37827-37843	BG59 FXA-F/H, BV10 WVD-H/J-M
VN 37843-37864	BV10 WWA/T/C-H/J-P/R/S/B/U/X, WVY/Z
VN 37865-37888	BF10 LSZ, LTA, BV10 WVP/R-T, BK10 MEV, MFA/E/N/F/J, BF10 LSO/U/V/X/Y, LTE/J, BV10 WVN/O/U/W/X
VN 37889	BK10 MFO
VN 37890-37942	BF60 UUA/B, UTZ, UUD/C/E/J/G/K/H/L/N/M/O/R/P/T/S/X/Y BF60 UUV/Z, BF60 VHP/R/V/U/W, UUW, VHT/X, VJA, VHY, VJC/K/J/E, VHZ, VJG/D/L/U/V, UVB/A/D/G/H/C/E, VJN/M/O/P
VN 37943	BK10 MFZ
VN 36101-36165	BJ11 DSE/Z/U, DTF, DSV, DTV/Y/O, DUV/A, DVH/F/P/M/L, DUU, DVK/C, DSY, DRZ, DSO, DTK/X/U, DVG, DUY, DVA/B/O/N/R, DSX, DTN/Z, DUH, DVV/W/T/U, DZX, EBP, EAM/F/X, EBG/L, EAK/W/O, EBD/C, EAE, DVX, EAA, DZZ/Y, EAC/G/P/Y, EBA/K/M/O/N
VN 37944-37951	BL61 ACY/X, ADU, ACZ, ADV, ADO/X/Z
VN 37952-37974	BN61 MWZ, MXB/A/E/D/H/C/F/G/L/K/J/P/M/O/R-U, BN61 MXY/X/W/V, BG61 SXK, BN61 MYA/B, BG61 SXJ/M/L/N/O/P/R
VN 36291-36295	BX12 CVO/M/K/L/P
VN 37988-37996	BF62 UYB/A/C/E/D/G/H/J/K

Date	Deliveries	Licensed for Service
09.09	VN 37774, 37775	
11.09	VN 37776-37803	VN 37773, 33777, 37778, 37780, 37782-37790, 37791-37796, 37800-37802 (**ON**)
12.09	VN 37804, 37805	VN 37774-37776, 37779, 37781, 37797-37799, 37803 (**ON**)
01.10	VN 37806-37820	VN 37804, 37805 (**NP**)
02.10	VN 37821-37835	VN 37806-37826 (**NP**), VN 37827-37829, 37831, 37832, 37834, 37835 (**LI**)
03.10	VN 37836-37846, 38748-37864	VN 37830, 37833, 37836-37842 (**LI**) VN 37843-37846, 37848-37864 (**NP**)
04.10	VN 37865-37888	VN 37865-37871, 37877-37885 (**HS**)
05.10	VN 37847, 37889	VN 37872-37876, 37886-37888 (**HS**), VN 37847, 37889 (**NP**)
07.10	VN 37943	
09.10	VN 37890-37904	
10.10	VN 37905-37942	VN 37890-37942 (**WJ**)
03.11	VN 36108, 36121-36125, 36133, 36134	
04.11	VN 36101-36107, 36109-36120, 36126-36132, 36135-36140, 36148, 36150, 36153-36158	VN 36101-36140, 36148, 36150, 36153-36158 (**LI**)
05.11	VN 36141-36145, 36147, 36149, 36151, 36152, 36159-36165	VN 36141-36145, 36147, 36149, 36151, 36152, 36159-36165 (**LI**)
06.11	VN 36146	VN 36146 (**LI**)
12.11	VN 37952-37962	VN 37952-37956, 37958-37962 (**X**)
01.12	VN 37944-37946, 37963-37974	VN 37953, 37957, 37963-37969, 37972, 37974 (**X**)
02.12	VN 37947-37951, 37975	VN 37970, 37971, 37973-37984 (**X**) VN 37944-37951 (**NP**)
05.12	VN 36291-36295	VN 36291-36295 (**AS**)
09.12	VN 37988-37995	VN 37988-37995 (**X**)
10.12	VN 37996	VN 37996 (**X**)

Disposals

31.03.12　VN 37804-37841, 37843, 37845, 37846, 37848, 37856-37858, 37944-37951 to London General

22.06.13　VN 37773-37803, 37865-37942 to Metroline
VN 36101-36165, 36291-36295, 37842, 37844, 37847, 37849-37855, 37859-37864, 37943, 37952-37984 and 37988-37996 to Tower Transit

Tower Transit

VN, VH and MV classes

Upon its formation on 22 June 2013, Tower Transit could field 129 VN-class Volvo B9TLs inherited from First London. These operated from Westbourne Park (route 295), Lea Interchange (routes 25 and 58) and Atlas Road (route 266).

The new logo, not unlike a cricket ball (with tampered seam?) made its appearance quickly, and the esoteric First numbering system was retained and in the event added to with quirks of its own.

Little happened across the rest of 2013 as the company found its feet, the only event of note being the treatment in October of VN 37952 to an ad exhorting tourists to visit Malaysia, and its subsequent removal in December. A lone transfer took VN 37943 and its special features to Lea Interchange in March 2014

Afer a most uneventful first year, expansion was on the cards when in June Tower Transit was awarded the contract for the 212,

Below: **Six weeks since the takeover and Lea Interchange's VN 36137 (BJ11 DVW) has received its new Tower Transit fleetnames; the date is 7 July 2013 and the location is Stratford bus station.** *Author*

hitherto operated by CT Plus. In September it placed an order for eleven Volvo B5LH hybrids with the revised Wrightbus Gemini 3 bodywork, and also applied for permission to source a new garage in the Enfield area for further single-deck contracts it had won for implementation at the same time as that of the 212.

In July VN 36105 was given an ad for Bulmers cider, exchanging it two months later for a David Gandy underwear advert.

VN 36139 was off the road with accident damage between 5 August and 8 October.

On 18 November the acquisition of a handful of former Stagecoach Tridents (classified TALs by Tower Transit) allowed VNs 37954 and 37961 to transfer from Westbourne Park to Lea Interchange, where they in turn would allow an equivalent number of DNs to add capacity to the 308, which was outgrowing its Darts in spite of three having been added over the year.

VN 37963, this time an Atlas Road motor, was another accident victim and was repaired at a body shop in Aylesford in Kent; VN 37952 regained red in December. VNs 36155 and 36165 were given ads for Invesco in January 2015.

2015 began with the delivery of the 212's new buses, coded VH 38101-38111 and featuring the new interior of green handrails and dark green seats. Two of them missed the 1 March deadline for their 64-registrations to stick and were re-registered with new 15-plates, blowing the otherwise orderly sequence. VH 38104 was tried out on the 30 on 17 and 19 February, though the 212 didn't start until 7 March. More TALs allowed three more VNs to head to Lea Interchange.

More ads in February affected VN 36111 (Pepsi Max Cherry) and VN 36154 (Pistachio Nuts). VN 36155 regained red in May.

Left: **The 212 was taken over from CT Plus on 7 March 2015 and eleven new Volvo B5LHs with Wright's refreshed Gemini 3 bodywork were delivered for it. Here at Walthamstow Central ten days after the start date is VH 38102 (BL64 MHE).** *Author*

12 May saw VN 36146 misjudge the Bow Flyover and hit it, whilst VN 37842 (visiting the 212, as did some B9TLs since its takeover) garnered its own newspaper headlines when it hit a cyclist and passers-by lifted the bus off the trapped bike, like Superman.

In June VNs 36111 and 36154 lost their ads. Between 10 and 28 August the 58 required a boost and Westbourne Park despatched four VNs (37956, 37959, 37960 and 37962) to Lea Interchange to provide it.

As companies gain tenders, so they can lose them too, and on 31 October the 295 passed to Metroline. This in theory released two dozen VNs, which were envisaged as taking over the 28 from its ageing VNWs, but

Below: **On 17 March 2015 two of the 212's new fleet are seen at Chingford, VH 38108 (BF15 KFU) on its way out and VH 38102 (BL64 MHE) having just arrived.** *Author*

Above: **The 25's batch of VNs 36101-36165 were joined during 2015 by earlier examples, allowing for a bit of variety. VN 37953 (BN61 MXB) is carrying one of the most unsightly T-side adverts with enormous leg blocking out half the lower saloon as it swings out of Stratford bus station on 18 February 2016.** Author

for the moment they allowed the acquired TALs to depart. They would serve as refurbishment cover when the 25's massive batch went through the process to cement the company's retention of this relentlessly busy trunk route. Another important retention was of the 328, and in October 25 more VHs were ordered. This time they would have the new and distinctly controversial angular redesigned front.

September saw two of the 58's reinforcements head home and October saw VN 36133 given an ad for Hungry House, an online takeaway delivery aggregator; it lasted until January. In November seven of the newest eight VNs were transferred to Atlas Road and took up service on the 28. Unusually, the Boxing Day complement on the 212 was VN-operated rather than the customary VHs.

Right: **Another one of the 61-reg new entrants to the 25 was VN 37962 (BN61 MXK), put into Lea Interchange to serve an increase to the 58. Carrying white-on-black blinds as was now the standard since the appearance of Borismasters, this bus is seen entering the bus station at Stratford on 5 June 2016.** Author

The 328's new fleet of VHs commenced delivery on 27 February 2016 and began working out of Atlas Road on 21 March. They were capable of visiting the 28 and 31 and sometimes did; a far rarer strange working was of the 212's VHs to the 25. The new VHs displaced VNs (and DNs) to Lea Interchange to provide cover as the 25's existing fleet got started going through Hants & Dorset trim. The refurbishments could be identified at a glance, not only by their new seating (though the handrails remained turquoise), but by their slightly smaller fleetnumber transfers without the serifs of the previous ones.

Tower Transit had been part of a complicated set of loans that had allowed CT Plus to bed in on the 26, one of its former routes; in order to supply DNs on loan it hired Tridents from Stagecoach. Once CT Plus's own new Enviro400H City double-deckers were in place, Lea Interchange now took back its DNs to use on the 69 and let the VNs borrowed from Atlas Road return home. As VNs had visited the 26, so did they repeat those visits on the 69, whilst the 308 was predominantly double-deck now to reflect sheer demand.

Tower Transit had definitely taken to the Volvo B5LH, given that all double-deck orders were hybrids by 2016, but for the award of route 13, the retention of the 308 and a three-bus top-up to the 58, it chose the cheap-but-cheerful MCV EvoSeti. The 13 was actually a sneaky renumbering of the 82, gained on tender from Metroline and altered to cut out the vital Oxford Street corridor in spite

of passengers' need for a route into central London. This was only the herald of brutal cuts which would threaten to hack London into two separate parts across Oxford Street.

In October 2016 an ad for the Austrian ski resort of Zillertal was applied to VN 36161.

Finally for 2016, the refurbishment programme to the 25's VNs was almost at its end, only a dozen remaining to be done by the end of the year.

The EvoSetis started arriving in January, classified MV 38201-38251. The first thirty-five were for Westbourne Park's assumption of the 13 on 1 April, though one turned out on the 23 on 4 March and regular appearances continued thereafter. The rest were intended for the 308 and 58 at Lea Interchange, the latter's share comprising three top-ups and all entering service between 18 April and 10 May.

Left: **Tower Transit has developed a liking for the EvoSeti-bodied variety of the Volvo B5LH, and the first of 51 ordered in 2017 began turning out on the 23 at Westbourne Park in advance of the company's acquisition of the 13. On 21 March 2017 MV 38209 (LJ17 WRN) halts at the pedestrian crossing at Marble Arch. The 23 itself is to be taken out of central London altogether before long, severing the already precarious bus links from the West End to the City.** *Author*

Above: **From 1 April 2017 the 13 effectively became the 82, to assuage the fears of Londoners that such a low-numbered route would be so abitrarily removed. It also passed to Tower Transit, with 34 of the new MCV EvoSeti-bodied Volvo B5LHs coded MV. Leaving Golders Green is MV 38224 (LJ17 WSD) on 3 April.** *Author*

Right: **Following the conversion of the 308 to MV operation, Lea Interchange's MV 38246 (LJ17 WTW) sets off from Wanstead on 10 May 2017.** *Author*

Atlas Road closed on 1 July, and part of the transfers to (or back to) Westbourne Park included 36 VNs (with routes 28 and 266) and 25 VHs with the 328). The 266 wasn't to stay with Tower Transit much longer, however, passing to Metroline West on the 29th. Rather than use the displaced five-year-old VNs to displace the remaining VNWs on the 23 and 31, it returned them off lease, a penny-pinching strategy rewarded by the announcement of the loss of the 31 for 2018 implementation!

Above: **From time to time the 25's VNs pop up on the 212, as shown by VN 36112 (BJ11 DVF) at Walthamstow Central on 27 August 2017. The blinds have been redone with thinner and rather less attractive numbers.** *Author*

During July two VNs received ads; VN 36113 for the London Metropolitan University and VN 36128 for Avocado, the latter lasting until October.

After a spell of quiet, punctuated by isolated disposals and returns off lease, VN 36113 lost its advert in April 2018. Finally for this account, the loss of the 30 to Metroline on 23 June stopped the appearance of VNs on that route.

Right: **Carnival weekend always produces oddments, and 2017 saw a new variation when Tower Transit used new MVs spare from the 13 on Sundays to add to the 328. Here at Harrow Road, Prince of Wales on Monday 29 August is MV 38203 (LJ17 WRD).** *Author*

Above: **The 28 replaced its VNWs with VNs once they became available from the loss of the 295, and here passing Westbourne Park garage on 24 September 2017 is VN 37990 (BF62 UYC). This route once again works out of Westbourne Park.** *Author*

Registrations

VH 38101-38111	BF15 KFE, BL64 MHE/F/J/K/M-N, BF15 KFU, BL64 MHU/V/X
VH 38112-38136	BU16 UXB/D/A/C/E/H/F/G/M/P/N/J/R/K/O/L/T/S/Z/Y/W, BU16 UYA, UXX, UYB, UXV
MV 38201-38251	LJ17 WRA/C-G/K/L/N-P/R/T-V, WSE/F/K/L/W/Y, WRW/X, WSD/N/O/U/V/X/Z, WTA/C-F/M-P/R/T-V/K/W-Z

Date	Deliveries	Licensed for Service
02.15	VH 38101-38111	VH 38102-38107, 38109-38111 (**LI**)
03.15		VH 38101, 38108 (**LI**)
03.16	VH 38112-38131	VH 38112-38117, 38119-38121 (**AS**)
04.16	VH 38132-38136	VH 38118, 38122-38136 (**AS**)
02.17	MV 38203, 38209, 38210	
03.17	MV 38201, 38204-38208, 38211-38235	MV 38201-38207, 38209-38235 (**X**)
04.17	MV 38236-38251	MV 38236-38246, 38248, 38249 (**LI**)
05.17		MV 38247, 38250, 38251 (**LI**)

Acquired

22.06.13	VN 36101-36165, 36291-36295, 37842, 37844, 37847, 37849-37855, 37859-37864, 37943, 37952-37984 and 37988-37996 from First London

Disposals

08.17	VN 36292-36295, 37964, 37966, 37968, 37977, 37981
10.17	VN 36291, 37963, 37965, 37967, 37969-37973, 37975, 37976, 37978-37980, 37983, 37984
04.18	VN 37974, 37982

Metroline

VW, VWH and VMH classes

Metroline had been a regular Volvo customer, taking as many B7TLs as it did Dennis Tridents, and would continue to alternate its orders between each manufacturer's next-generation product.

In July 2009 the company was awarded the 237, which it had been running out of Brentford since that firm's original owner, Armchair, was bought out. TPs were the current staple, but in October 22 of the then all-new Wrightbus Gemini 2-bodied Volvo B9TL were ordered, reflecting confidence in the new model which had fought off noise problems to garner solid orders, Metroline being the third London contractor after First and Go-Ahead to take examples.

Subject to Metroline's quirky numbering system, in which class codes only preceded a consecutive number regardless of type, the new B9TLs were numbered VW 1034-1055, following on from DE 1033, the last of a batch of Enviro200s. VW 1034 arrived at Metroline's CELF facility on 30 January 2010, not long after the 237's new contract had kicked in on 9 January, and the rest followed in February and March, by which time the 59-marks booked for them had to be replaced by 10-regs. Seventeen more VWs were ordered at this point, though it wasn't yet clear as to where they would be deployed.

The service debut of the 237's new VWs was 27 March, with the whole batch running

Right: **New VWs replaced the TEs already bedded in on the E2 in order to standardise Brentford on Volvo B9TLs. On 7 May 2012 VW 1065 (LK60 AEM) awaits the off at Ealing Broadway.** *Author*

by April. Here it was decided to allocate the 17 new VWs (1056-1072) to Brentford as well, taking over the E2's recently-installed TEs and allowing the garage to standardise on Volvo B9TLs. The VWs were already visiting the E2, and also the E8, in lieu of that route's unreliable Tempo hybrids.

VWs 1056-1072 were built in July and August and were shipped to Heysham beginning on 2 September. They began entering service on the E2 from the 30th, allowing its TEs to leave for Cricklewood. A new venture for the VWs from this point was the 190.

In December 2010 the 105 was won from First London and an order placed for thirty more VWs, eighteen of which would be furnishing the 16-strong PVR of the 105 from 2 July 2011. The fate of the balance was made clear when the 79's award to Metroline was announced in April, another win from First. The batch started arriving at CELF on 17 May, but an interesting herald of the future came on the same day with the loan of Volvo B5LH hybrid BK10 MGV for tests up and down the 16 and 82 road shadowing service buses.

Above: **Both batches of Brentford VWs soon turned out on the 190, and on 7 May 2012 VW 1035 (LK10 BXC) has arrived at Richmond on one such journey.** *Author*

Left: **The E8 at Brentford was also fair game for VWs, and on 18 August 2012 we see VW 1064 (LK60 AEL) pulling into Ealing Broadway after a trip a Tempo hybrid couldn't manage.** *Author*

Right: **The new order on the 105 is personified on 10 July 2011 by VW 1185 (LK11 CXV) at Heathrow.** *Author*

As the latest batch of VWs arrived, twelve more were ordered; these were intended to displace TEs from the 297 at Perivale West and then cover the 79. This extended the numbering sequence to VW 1216. To get them ready for this, a number of the 105's incoming VWs were run in on the 297 from 21 June, so that TEs could go to Holloway to address shortages there. A gap ensued before the balance arrived, but all were ready to assume the 297 starting from 20 August.

The 79's contract commenced on 26 November, and VWs 1205-1216 (starting the new European Whole Vehicle Type specification that extended their length from 10.4m to 10.5m) were delivered in time for a seamless takeover. This route ran from the original Perivale rather than the one that came with the acquisition of Thorpe's. It wasn't a month before the new buses started wandering to the 7, that route's SEL-class Scanias paying back the favour.

Right: **VW 1183 (LK11 CXT) reposes at Ealing Broadway on 7 May 2012, waiting to set off on another rounder on the 297. VW operation on this route did battle with Scanias during the decade.** *Author*

Left: **VW 1216 (LK61 BNO) swings into Edgware bus station at the end of another journey on the 79 on 28 July 2012. By this time it was operating out of the 'other' Perivale to the one whose code was still carried on the side.** *Author*

Metroline's 43 and 134 routes probing north from Archway are the jewel in the company's crown, and their retention on tender in October prompted a massive order for new buses. Sixty-four new VWs (1243-1306) were to furnish these two routes (though the 43's 'new bus' requirement was only partial) as well as the W7, won back at the same time. VW 1215 was sent to Holloway in January for type training in advance of deliveries, which began on 9 March, and on 2 April three went into service, replacing the

Below: **After the elegantly proportioned 10.6m VPLs and TPLs, the new order of VWs on Holloway's 43 and 134 seemed rather ordinary. On 27 May 2012, not long after entering service, VW 1255 (LK12 AUX) rounds Muswell Hill Broadway.** *Author*

Left: **The VW class's takeover of the 134 is represented at Archway by Holloway's VW 1286 (LK12 AOT) on 30 November 2013.** *Author*

Below left: **Completing the trio of Holloway VW deployments in 2012 was the W7, on which VW 1264 (LK12 AEZ) is seen at Muswell Hill on 27 May 2012.** *Author*

TPs in situ since 1999. As well as the 43, 134 and W7, they were soon to be spotted on the 390, plus (from early June) night routes N5 and N20. Later they added the N91 and day 91 to their quiver. And these wouldn't be the only VWs into Holloway in 2012, as in May the most prestigious of prestige routes, the 24, was awarded to Metroline for a second tilt, ex-London General. Twenty-four more were ordered (VW 1365-1388), plus five of the new B5LH hybrid (VWH 1360-1364).

In two stages on 9 and 23 June, Perivale garage was mothballed and its routes transferred out; the 79 passed to Perivale West on the latter date and took VWs 1205-1216 with it, enabling them to join the others on the 105 and 297.

From 8 July VWs 1290-1300 from the ongoing Holloway batch were seconded for Olympics work, which required they go around anonymous, without fleetnames. The last two of the order arrived after Wrights resumed work after the annual July shutdown, having been built before the workforce was despatched on their holidays.

Having already won the 24, Metroline retained the 52 when this tranche was announced, and proceeded to place another order for Volvo double-deckers. This time, a hybrid component was mandatory and in a larger proportion, so the split was fifteen B9TLs (VW 1393-1407) and twelve B5LHs

Left: **The 390 was still operated by the VPLs that had replaced its Routemasters after 'Black Friday' 3 September 2014, but Holloway's new VWs soon made regular appearances, exemplified in Oxford Street on 16 June 2013 by VW 1267 (LK12 AFU).** *Author*

(VWH 1408-1419). Four more VWs (1389-1392) would give the unfortunate 4 at least a proportion of new vehicles; it hadn't had a full complement of brand new buses since Ms one-manned it in 1985! Finally, one last Volvo was added to the order to top up Holloway, and this would take the number VW 1468, following on from booked numbers for TEs and TEHs.

From the date of the W7's contract renewal (18 August), the route was specified for VWs at the expense of the 43, which didn't require as many contractually and thus reverted to mixed TPL/VPL operation to go with the mandated proportion of new VWs. When the newest VWs came back from Olympics duty in September, they helped top up the 43.

The 24's five VWHs arrived in October, well in time for the route's assumption on 10 November, although existing Holloway VWs had to help out until all the new buses were in stock. The hybrids immediately wandered to the 43, 134 and W7, showing that they were not so niche now as to need special treatment through restriction to certain routes.

Above: **The 24, it seemed, couldn't stick with an operator past five years and on 10 November 2012 it passed from London General back to Metroline at Holloway, using VWs and VWHs. At first existing Holloway B9TLs like VW 1295 (LK12 ARZ, *right*), joined the new deliveries like VW 1373 (LK62 DNE, *left*), seen at the 24's Hampstead Heath stand on 25 November.** *Author*

Left: **VW 1383 (LK62 DSE) pauses at Trafalgar Square on 25 November.** *Author*

Right: **After the 24, it was the turn of the 52 to add VWs and VWHs, and on 26 August 2013 Willesden's VW 1397 (LK62 DVG) is seen at Notting Hill Gate.** *Author*

Next up was the 52's batch of VWs and VWHs, and in December Holloway sent VW 1388 to Willesden to get that garage started on training drivers and engineers. Conversion began on 5 February 2013 and continued over the month, displacing VPs to Harrow Weald. The last three VWs, plus VWH 1413,

were re-registered with 13-marks replacing their booked 62-regs. Both VWs and VWHs soon saw fit to wander to the 6, 98, 260 and 460 at Willesden.

As it turned out, the tenure of Volvos on the 24 was to be short-lived, as the route was chosen to be the inaugural route for the LT

Below: **The 52's hybrid element is represented in this Victoria shot of 24 February 2013 by Willesden's VWH 1415 (LK62 DWU).** *Author*

class of Borismaster, or New Bus for London, call it what you will. This took place on 22 June in one shot, cascading the five VWHs to Willesden to join their newer counterparts on the 52. The VWs were stood down for the moment, but a greater purpose was at hand for them, because 22 June was also the day Metroline doubled its size through the acquisition from FirstGroup of five of its garages and all their buses, renaming the new arm Metroline West. Of Alperton, Hayes, Greenford, Willesden Junction and Uxbridge, the first, second and fourth fielded 109 Volvo B9TLs compatible with Metroline's existing VWs, and indeed brought what first termed VNs into Metroline's own fleet in a grand renumbering.

Based at Alperton for the 83, VNs 37773-37803 became VWs 1752-1782. Hayes's route 427 fleet of VNs 37865-37889 were renumbered VW 1817-1841 and Willesden Junction's large fleet for the 18, comprising VNs 37890-37942, became VWs 1842-1894. Fleetnames appeared quicker at some garages than others, but the new order was in evidence by the autumn and First was forgotten.

The VWs replaced from the 24 by LTs (plus seven more from Holloway's earlier intake) marked the first inter-company co-operation between the new Metroline siblings, as they were earmarked for the double-decking of the 245 at Alperton starting in late July.

Above: **VWH 1409 (LK62 DWD) is seen visiting the 6 on 17 August 2013.** *Author*

Below: **VW 1831 (BF10 LSV) at Uxbridge on 14 July was once VN 37879.** *Author*

Top left: **VW 1780 (LK59 FCV) at Golders Green on 14 July 2013 was the renumbered First VN 37801.** *Author*

Top right: **Willesden Junction's VW 1870 (BF60 VHT) at Elgin Avenue on 26 August 2013, was new as First VN 37918.** *Author*

Above left: **Another 18 bus on Carnival diversion is VW 1842 (BF60 UUA), ex-VN 37890.** *Author*

Above right: **The 24's LT conversion released VWs to double-deck the 245; here at Golders Green on 1 April 2014 is VW 1376 (LK62 DNX).** *Author*

Right: **VW 1468 (LK13 BJE) was a top-up for Holloway, and is seen setting off from Archway on 30 November 2013.** *Author*

After these upheavals, the rest of 2013 proved quiet. Although they did not know it at the time, Metroline had purchased their last B9TL, as hybrids were now in the ascendancy, led by the innovative if controversial Borismaster.

The Metroline and Metroline West VWs may have looked alike (interior decor notwithstanding), but they had different cab layouts, and a handful of transfers effected in August reflected this. For the most part, the vehicles stuck to where they were delivered, though four of the earlier ex-Holloway VWs intended for Alperton were sent to Brentford instead, to see off the last TPs based there.

Those now bedded in at Alperton after a protracted conversion of the 245 started popping up on the 487.

On 7 December Holloway converted a second route to LT operation, but this didn't stop the odd VW from getting out when Borismasters failed; when that was the case, they remained OPO.

2014 began with the award to and retention by Metroline of the 7 (and N7), with new buses to replaced its Scanias. These were firmed up in January as 23 Volvo B5LHs with Wrightbus bodies; more VWHs. But in the interim, the bodybuilder had revised the design to cut the upper-deck window height

down. They would also take Metroline stock numbers into the two thousands after the First acquisitions had propelled them there.

All-over ads came late to Metroline VWs, but in November VWs 1399 and 1407 gained ads for Saxony and the following March VWs 1401 and 1406 took on vinyls for Schuh shoes. VW 1406 reverted to red in May, VW 1399 and 1407 in July.

The 7's VW batch began arriving at CELF on 22 May and the first entered service at Perivale West on 25 June, but playing it safe on school route 611 for a week untl squadron entry on the 7 got started in earnest on 1 July. The SELs stayed put, transferring first to the 297 and displacing nine of its newer

VWs to Holloway. As the 7's VWHs entered traffic, another order was placed for 38 more to take over the 34 and 125, two important tendering gains from Arriva London North and both due for takeup on 8 November. At this point it was wondered whether it would be more effective to put VWH 2024-2061 on fellow Potters Bar route 82 and cascade TEs, thus fulfilling central London emissions requirements.

In August VWs 1243-1248 left Brentford and struck up a new allocation at Harrow Weald, to fulfil not only a four-bus boost to the 140 from 30 August, but the simultaneous acquisition of school route 340 from Arriva the Shires.

On 13 and 14 September Holloway VWs and VPLs operated four special double-deck workings on the 214 between Moorgate and Camden Town, carrying slipboards.

VW 1407 gained its second advert in September, this time for David Gandy underwear; it wore it until November.

Not all the VWHs for the 34 and 125 were in place at Potters Bar for the 34's 8 November start date, in spite of deliveries having started on 21 October and VWH 2015 sent to train staff, so TEs were gathered together to start off the 34. Even so, VWHs were in evidence from the first day.

The year was rounded out by three garages' worth of new strange workings not seen hitherto; at Holloway VWs on the 4, 17 and 271, at Perivale West VWHs on the 79, 90, 105 and 297 and at Harrow Weald VWs on the 182.

Above: **The 34's VWHs shared it with TEs at first; here at Arnos Grove on 27 November 2014 is Potters Bar's VWH 2041 (LK64 EHJ).** *Author*

Below: **The next step for the new VWHs was the 125, also put into Potters Bar. Passing Southgate on 27 February 2015 is VWH 2029 (LK64 EDP).** *Author*

and 98 instead, even though this total would only cover one of the pair.

On 31 January the 125 was commenced out of Potters Bar, with enough VWHs delivered to furnish it alongside the inevitable few TEs. The last two, VWHs 2052 and 2057, entered service on 8 April. The new Volvos did make it to the 82 from time to time, though in ones and twos only.

VW 1291 received an ad for Pepsi Max in March. The first 'route 7' VWH to gain an all-over ad was VWH 2002 in February, extolling Peru. The diverted Willesden batch, meanwhile, were all built by April and all but six of the 34 were delivered in May ready for allocation in June.

In April the award for the 295 was announced; Metroline would be having it from 14 November and in May 23 more VWHs were placed on order. This time they would be to a revised frontal design, as Wrights had phased in its unnamed and extremely controversial angular new body that was drawing comment up and down the industry and enthusiast bodies alike.

Willesden's new VWHs (2088-2121) began entering service on 15 June, sticking mostly to the 6 but also working on the 52 and 98. VWH 2023 from the tail end of the 7's batch joined them after having been allocated as a trainer. All were delivered by June even if their appearance dragged out interminably.

Above and below: Two of the 6's new Volvo B5LH hybrids, Willesden's VWH 2115 (LK15 CXP) at Trafalgar Square on 10 September 2015 and VWH 2095 (LK15 CWT) at Edgware Road on 10 October 2015. *Both: Author*

2015 began brightly for Metroline, with two wins that let them keep the 245 and 460 on the promise of new buses. 34 new VWHs were ordered on this basis, but Metroline's propensity to allocate new vehicles away from their intended contracts came into play when it was decided to switch them to the 6

Above: **Spring sunshine bathes Warren Street's junction on 15 May 2015 as Willesden Junction's VW 1880 (BF60 VJD) happens across on the 18, its earlier identity as First VN 37928 long forgotten.** *Author*

VW 1291 lost its Pepsi Max ad in June and VWH 2002 reverted to red in August. In advance of the delivery of the 295's VWHs to Willesden Junction, VWHs 2094 and 2097 from the 6's batch were sent there for training before entering service on their intended routes. Existing VWs at Holloway were forced to sub for defective Borismasters in large numbers during the summer, their use in this fashion being restricted to the 390 rather than the prestige 24.

Even though the 6's complement of VWHs had all still to enter service, the 295's own batch had not made it on time

Left: **When Borismasters failed (and this was far from uncommon as Holloway got to grips with two batches of the complicated and sophisticated vehicles) VWs substituted, but only on the 390, which was considered far lower profile than the 24. Crossing Marble Arch on 9 December 2015, therefore, is VW 1216 (LK61 BNO). It's still carrying Perivale West codes from an earlier stint there.** *Author*

Right: Holloway's VW 1300 (LK12 AUF) carries its Hungry House advert across London Bridge on the morning of 19 December 2015. *Author*

Below and below right: Differences between Gemini 3 rears as Wrightbus tinkered with the design; happily, the rear of the redesign is rather more conservative than the front! Illustrated are VWH 2003 (LK14 FAJ) at Oxford Circus on 9 November 2015 (*left*) and VWH 2140 (LK65 ECC) from the 295's batch at Clapham Junction on 22 December (*right*). *Author*

for 14 November, so some shuffles had to be executed to accompany the nine VWHs that were available to Willesden Junction. Holloway sent five VWs, Potters Bar two VWHs and Willesden four of its VWHs that were already running; together with the five still awaited at Willesden, a service was put together. All were delivered by the end of November and the last entered service on 26 December. Occasionally a VW could be found wandering over from the 18.

Two VWs received all-over ads in November; VW 1262 for Campo Viejo and VW 1300 for Hungry House. VW 1290's ad for Dubai was particularly short-lived.

A similar issue to that of the 295 was experienced when the 307 was acquired on 12 December for operation by Potters Bar, but this time it was late-arriving Borismasters that were to blame; they were supposed to displace TEHs from Cricklewood's 168 to further cascade TEs, but in the event the four

Gemini 3 VWHs that had been standing in on the 295 were loaned to Potters Bar for a few weeks, after which they finally entered service at Willesden. 2015 was rounded off with VW 1300 losing its ad in December and VW 1262 regaining red in January.

The contracts operated by Harrow Weald have always meant life or death for that garage, and the end of 2016 saw the former secured with a bang, for not only were the 140 and 182 retained, but the 114 won from neighbouring Sovereign. Thus, a whopping 77 new VWHs were ordered for delivery by the start of the new terms in August.

VW 1399 gained and lost an ad for Children's Cancer , VWH 1360 gained one for Doom, the first-person shooter video game and VW 1291 gained one for Cent-Intel.

One well-established grouping of VWs was broken up on 28 May when the E8 at Brentford was specified to convert to full-time double-deck operation and seventeen VWs were transferred for this role from Holloway, replaced there by LTs taking over the 91. The E8 was extended at the same time to Hounslow.

In June Perivale West's VWH 2008 from the 7 batch gained an advert for T-Systems.

Enough work had now been recouped by Metroline to make reopening Perivale feasible, and on 6 August in went the 7, 79 and N7 from Perivale West with their buses, plus the 245 from Alperton. This precluded VWH appearances on the 90, 105 and 297

The end of June saw the delivery commence of VWHs 2167-2243; as it turned out, there wouldn't be enough space in Harrow Weald for the 114, so it was to be put into Uxbridge. Enough had come for that task at least, spanning Wrights' summer holiday

Above: **Seen on the E8's new stretch of route to Hounslow on 29 July 2016 is VW 1212 (LK61 BNF), transferred from Holloway to Brentford.** *Author*

Below: **Turning out on the 90 while it still could was Perivale West's VWH 2010 (LK14 FBD) at Hayes & Harlington on 28 May 2016.** *Author*

Right: **The 79 was reallocated on 6 August 2016 from Perivale West to Perivale; VW 1207 (LK61 BMY), however, is carrying Holloway codes as it leaves Edgware on 8 September.** *Author*

Below: **New blind standards developed during 2015 reduced the thickness of numbers and separated them, supposedly for easier reading but in reality rendering them unattractive; poor Johnston would turn in his grave if he saw what Perivale's VW 1210 (LK61 BNB) was carrying as it headed out of Golders Green on 11 September 2016. The 245 had been transferred from Alperton to Perivale on 6 August and thus merited new blinds.** *Author*

shutdown, but, aided by the loan for training of VWH 2128 from Willesden Junction, Harrow Weald put two new examples into service on 8 August, one each on the 140 and 182.

3 September marked the contract start date of the 140 and 182 and the takeover of the 114, the last mentioned's assumption by Uxbridge

VWHs having to bounce two routes out of that garage. Then on the 10th came the turn of the 83 to split in two, the main route falling back from the north to terminate at Alperton Garage, which continued to operate it and its new southern offshoot numbered 483, which continued after the overlap to forge new links to Harrow Bus Station. As well

Left: It was pretty clear by 2016 that Metroline had plumped for the Volvo B5LH over the Enviro400H; another order for VWHs was particularly huge, taking in 77 for the 114, 140 and 182. The 114's batch came first as they needed to take over the route from Sovereign, and on 11 September we see Uxbridge's VWH 2181 (LK16 DGE) entering Harrow town centre. *Author*

Left: The 83 had survived for many years over a length that had become less comfortable to cover through the mad traffic in parts of town like Wembley, so from 10 September 2016 it was cut in half. The day after the change, Alperton's VW 1269 (LK12 AFX), formerly of Holloway, is now going no further south than Alperton garage. *Author*

Left: Picking up the 83's southern section was new route 483, which was then projected onward to form useful new links to Harrow. This was also the responsbility of Alperton, whose indigenous VW 1782 (LK59 FCY) is seen arriving at Harrow on 11 September with its blinds already turned for the return journey. *Author*

as twelve VWs coming from Holloway after roundabout displacement by Borismasters, Harrow Weald gave up its VWs to Alperton to provide the general increase the split had produced.

VW 1300 and 1306 gained ads in July, the former for U-Switch and the latter for Zoopla. VW 1291 and VWH 1360 resumed

red livery in August. Two with a 'Z' theme in September were VW 1865 for Zillertal and VWH 2008 (ex-T-Systems) for Zoopla.

The autumn saw the continuing but very slow conversion of the 140 and 182 from VP, with the VWHs delivered after 1 September having to take on the new 66-registrations. All the new buses were delivered by the end of

October, but the conversion still hadn't been completed by the end of 2016, four stubborn examples remaining to be licensed. The new batches didn't wander, but Uxbridge put one out on the 607 on 12 November. Finally for 2016, VWH 1416 gained itself an all-over ad for India.

When it came to Volvo B5LHs, Metroline didn't do anything by halves; against contracts upcoming for the retention of the 17, 260 and 302 and the gain of the 120 from London United, a further 79 Gemini 3-bodied Volvo B5LHs were ordered, which would comprise VWHs 2266-2344. Immediately

Above: **There were only enough VWHs for the 6 after they were diverted from their intended deployment, but occasionally the 98's VPs are joined by newer Volvos. This one, however, is VWH 1409 (LK62 DWD) from the 52's fleet at Willesden, and it is seen at Marble Arch on 11 September 2016.** *Author*

Left: **Just your common-or-garden Holloway VW on the 134, wearing a rear ad for Essential Living. This one is VW 1279 (LK12 ALO), seen at the bottom of Tottenham Court Road on 6 November 2016, before expected road changes turn this busy thoroughfare back into a two-way street.** *Author*

Right: **The 427 was important enough to Metroline West that its loss to Abellio forced the closure of Hayes garage. On 14 November 2016 VW 1820 (BV10 WVR) poses between journeys at Uxbridge.** *Author*

Below: **More SNs needed to be replaced than there were VWs coming off the 427, so an extra number of Volvos transferred out of Holloway, their route 134 otherwise reallocated to Potters Bar with TEs. On 12 April VW 1281 (LK12 AMV) heads west past Ealing Common.** *Author*

after that a further order for eighteen was placed to cover the 4.

VWHs 2198 and 2225 were the last of the big batch of 2016 to enter service, in February 2017. VWH 2225 had been at Holloway training drivers in advance of the big batch to come. VW 1300 lost its U-Switch advert in February and VW 1865 advertising Zillertal similarly reverted to red. In March VW 1306 (Zoopla) and VWH 1416 (India) resumed red livery.

The loss of the 427 to Abellio on 8 April saw its VWs transferred to Greenford to replace the SNs from the 207; at the same time

Hayes was closed. Nonetheless, Uxbridge's VWH 2186 visited Hayes on 4 March and turned out on the 207. Additional VWs into Greenford were thirteen from Holloway.

VWH 2266 was delivered on 1 April 2017, coming through CELF first as is customary for Metroline. Existing VWs continued to pass through refurbishment, by this time comprising Brentford's contingent and the first of Alperton's original deliveries. The black detailing vanished from these buses upon repaint.

Definitely committed to the B5LH, Metroline ordered eighteen more for the 4 and in April splurged on seventy for not only the retained 6 and 98 but the 222, captured on

tender from London United. The 6, already fielding 15-reg VWHs, was rerouted on 17 June to take it via Park Lane and Piccadilly rather than the time-honoured Oxford Street, steadily being downgraded with the intent to pedestrianise.

The two VWHs in advert livery by April, 2008 (Zoopla) and 2010 (uSwitch) resumed red that month.

Prior to the takeup of route 120 on 17 June, Perivale West put one of its new VWHs into service on the 90 on 31 May, with others following, comprising VWHs 2266-2284.

The new buses of the VWH 2345-2432 batch ended up falling foul of TfL's obsession with continually renewing central London

routes in the name of emissions reduction, despite a lot of talk about doing the same for the suburbs. The 17's contingent (VWHs 2285-2304) were diverted to the 7 at Perivale (commencing on 27 July) so that its existing 14-reg VWHs could move to Holloway instead and take up the 17. Later in the summer, the new VWHs meant for the 260 and 302 at Willesden were already entering service on the 302 when they were whisked off that route and switched to the 6 and 98.

During July VWH 1413 was given an advert for City of Westminster College and VWH 2088 one for Avocado (which lasted until October). August saw Willesden's VWH 1364 also treated to the City of Westminster College ad.

On 16 September the 222 was indeed taken up, operating from a new outstation at Wallingford Road due to Uxbridge's being full. However, none of its intended batch had yet arrived, so a contingency plan was

Left: **Uxbridge took over the 222 on 16 September 2017, though the garage was now full so an off-site annex was founded. The intended VWHs were not yet in place, however, the supply having run dry over the summer works shutdown, so a complicated set of transfers was instituted which saw the 114's existing VWHs step in, themselves replaced by TEs and VWHs meant to be going into service at Willesden (and these buses themselves were diverted from their original deployments!). On 20 September at Uxbridge we see VWH 2182 (LK16 DGF).**
Author

mounted whereby incoming new VWHs, already with Willesden codes, were sent to Uxbridge for the 114 and its existing VWHs put onto the 222. Deliveries in September and October slowly put examples of the 114's batch (VWH 2345-2363) into Uxbridge, allowing Willesden's loans to go home, though still not to their correct 260 and 302.

In October VW 1873 was given an advert for Zillertal, carrying it until January 2018.

Below: **VWHs 2320 (LK17 DDU) and 2311 (LK17 DFG) are together at Ruislip on the afternoon of 20 September 2017, filling in on the 114 while that route's own buses got the 222 started. Slipboards have had to be the case, however.**
Author

Above: **Once again, the 6 and 98 were prioritised over the latest new buses' intended operations, making a nonsense of the contract terms. Instead of the 260 or 302, VWH 2307 (LK17 DFC) is seen on the 98, coming up to Marble Arch on 24 September 2017.** *Author*

Right: **Similarly, VWH 2310 (LK17 DFF) is rounding Marble Arch a little further round the roundabout on the same day.** *Author*

Above: **In August 2017 Willesden's VWH 1364 (LK62 DKE) from the 52's batch was given an all-over ad for the City of Westminster College, and on 24 September is seen taking it across Hyde Park Corner.** *Author*

The most severe route loss for some time took place on 11 November when the 18 was lost to London United. VWs 1846-1894 were stood down and returned off lease, even with much older buses still existing that they could have replaced.

The slowness of deliveries from Wright was enough to prompt Metroline to switch suppliers when it came time to order B5LHs for the 30, 31 and 274, retained (or, in the case of the 30, won from Tower Transit); these 66 would be bodied by MCV. This order was placed in January 2018.

A handful of Willesden VWHs found themselves fitted with orange lights beside their headlight clusters, which would flash in

Left: **Naturally, as soon as the big batch of VWHs arrived at Willesden for the 260 and 302, or rather the 6 and 98, they began turning out on the 52, as VWH 2329 (LK17 DCV) is doing when captured at the revamped environs of Victoria on 4 January 2018.** *Author*

time with audible alarms when passing along Oxford Street; extraordinarily irritating, and intended to be superfluous anyway when Oxford Street lost its buses, as was the plan. The balance of the VWHs into service indirectly finished off Holloway's VPs by 15 January and had reduced Willesden's own fleet of that type to four by April.

Another controversial experiment was route branding, and in January it came time for a scheme based on Hayes to follow one implemented in the Barkingside area the

previous summer. A handful of Harrow Weald VWHs (2188-2193 and 2237) participated for the 140, whose chosen colour was dark green, while the 90's B9TL participants in light pink were VWs 1175-1177.

In February VWHs 2105 and 2381 were given adverts for Oyster, boosting knowledge of its associated Hopper fare.

On 28 April the 31 was taken over on tender from Tower Transit, going into Perivale West with existing VWs sourced from reductions (ten each out of Holloway

Left: **The VWHs recently put into Holloway were capable of wandering off route when needed, and here at Moorgate on 25 February 2018 is VWH 2094 (LK15 CWR).** *Author*

Left: **By the beginning of 2018 the 260 and 302 at Willesden were at last seeing the buses that were purchased for them, but only after the VPs that had held out on these services were all but gone. On 25 February VWH 2315 (LK17 DFD) is seen setting off from Golders Green.** *Author*

Left: **The Hayes incarnation of a route-branding exercise was more attractive than the version implemented in 2017 on routes serving Barkingside; there were fewer buses with the treatment, enabling flexibility to be maintained (though the 140's small number of branded VWHs still managed to get out on the 182!) If you're sat in the front row, unfortunately, your view out is completely blocked on either side, as there's nowhere else physically to plaster the vinyls than on the windows. This is Harrow Weald's VWH 2193 (LK16 HZX) and it is seen at Hayes & Harlington station on 25 February 2018.** *Author*

Above: **The 90's chosen colour in the Hayes-area route branding scheme of 2018 was pink, as seen on refurbished VW 1175 (LK11 CXJ) at Hayes & Harlington Station on 22 May 2018.** *Author*

and seven from Willesden) rather than new vehicles as intended. The N7 was reallocated there from Perivale on the same day.

In April VWH 2315 was given an advert for Green Bus.

23 June was a good day for Metroline Volvo B5LHs; first the 30 was picked up on tender from Tower Transit and set going from King's Cross with the first of the new MCV-bodied VMHs. The rest added an upper deck back

Right: **Willesden's VWH 2327 (LK67 CYH) is flashing its acid strobes fit to burst, though there's barely anyone in Oxford Street on the morning of 3 June 2018 to see them; an ominus portent of the future, if plans to close this critical shopping thoroughfare to bus traffic are put into practice.** *Author*

Left: **VW 1190 (LK11 CYA) was already in residence at Perivale West to accept the 31 on 28 April 2018. It still seems odd to see this route turning right out of Notting Hill Gate, rather than left and then right again to support the 28, but that's just what this bus is doing when seen on 3 June.** *Author*

Left: **Fighting its way through afternoon peak traffic at Burnt Oak on 8 June is Willesden's VWH 2307 (LJ17 DFC) on the 302.** *Author*

Left: **VWH 2315 (LJ17 DFO) was another 302 out that day from Willesden, and is seen taking its 'Green Bus' TfL advert through Burnt Oak.** *Author*

Above: **The 30 went over to Metroline as planned on 23 June 2018, putting into service Metroline's first MCV EvoSeti-bodied Volvo B5LHs. King's Cross's VMH 2479 (LK18 AOE) is seen at Baker Street on 1 July.** *Author*

to the 274 on the same day, also from King's Cross, but in this case tree pruning along the rest of the route had not been tackled. Until it was sorted out whose responsibility this relatively straightforward task was, which would have been carried out in times of old with dedicated tree-loppers constructed out of former buses, four of the new VMHs performed shortworkings between Marble Arch and the London Zoo on weekends only.

Right: **Somebody forgot to get the trees along Agar Grove pruned, TfL blaming Camden Council and vice versa; while these organisations bickered, a planned service cut went in on the 274 which made it even more necessary to get its new VMHs into service. Caught between the two, Metroline played it safe by putting the new double-deckers out on weekend shorts only as far as London Zoo, and when seen at Baker Street on 1 July 2018, VMH 2470 (LK18 ANP) has just come back from there.** *Author*

Registrations

VW 1034-1055	LK59 JJU, LK10 BXC-H/J/L-P/R/S/U-Z, BYA
VW 1056-1072	LK60 AEA-G/J/L-P/T-W
VW 1175-1204	LK11 CXJ/L-P/R-Z, CYA/E/F/H/J/L/O/P/S-V, LK61 BJE/F/J
VW 1205-1216	LK61 BMU/V/Y/Z, BNA/B/E/F/J/L/N/O
VW 1243-1306	LK12 AAF/J/N/U, ABF/O/X, ADU/V/X, AEA/B/F/G/T/U, AFO, AEW/Z, AFA/E/U/V/X, AHA/C/D/O/U/Z, AJX, AKN/O, ALO, AMO/V, ANF, AOA/L/O/T/X/Y, APF, APV, APZ, ARO/U/X/Z, ASZ, ATU/V, AUE/F/M/N/U/V/W/Y
VWH 1360-1364	LK62 DHX/Y, DJY/Z, DKE
VW 1365-1388	LK62 DKN/V, DLJ/O/V/X, DMV, DND/E/U/O/X, DOH, DPE/U/Y, DRV/Z, DSE/U/V, DTN/U/V
VW 1389-1404	LK62 DTZ, DUA/H/J/U, DVBC/F/G/H/J/L/O/P/R/U
VW 1405-1407	LK13 BHW/X/Y
VWH 1408-1419	LK62 DWA/D-F/J, LK13 BHZ, LK62 DWO/U/V/Y, DXF/G
VW 1468	LK13 BJE
VWH 2001-2023	LK14 FAA/F/J/M/O/U, FBA-G/J/L/N/O/U/V/X-Z, FCA
VWH 2024-2061	LK64 EDC/F/J/L/O/P/R/U/V/X, EHB-H/J/L-P/R-Z, EJA/C-G
VWH 2088-2121	LK15 CWD-G/O/P/R/T-Z, CXA-H/J/L-P/R-W
VWH 2122-2144	LK65 EAX/Y, EBA/C/D/F/G/J/L-P/U/C/X/Z, ECA/C/D, EOA-C
VWH 2167-2243	LK16 DFD-G/J/L/N-P/U/V/X-Z, DGE/F/O/V, HZC, DGX-Z, DHA, HZU-X, LK66 DWD, ENU-X, DWZ/U, LK16 DHE, LK66 DXA, DWW/X/E/Y/P, DXB/C, DWC/F, LK16 HZE-H/J/L-N/P/R-T, LK66 ENY, EOA-C, DWG/J/L-O, EOD-H/J/L/M/O
VWH 2266-2344	LK17 CZO/P/R-X, CXY, CZC-H/J/L-N, CYP/S-W/Y/Z, CZA/B, DFP/U/V/X-Z, DGF/O/U/V, DFA/C-G/J/L/N/O, DDJ/N/O/U/V/X-Z, DCF/O/U/V/X-Z, DDA/E/F, DAA/O/U, DBO/U/V/X-Z
VWH 2345-2432	LK67 CXB-H/J/L-P/R-Z, CYA/C/E-H/J/L, EKO/P/R/T-Z, ELC/H/J/O/U-X, EMF/J/V/X, ENC/E/F/H/J/L-P/R/T-Y, EOA-H/J/L/M/O/P/R-W
VMH 2433-2498	LK18 AFA/E/F/J/N/O/U/V/X-Z, AGO/U/V/X-Z, AHA/C-F, AKN-P/U/V/X-Z, ALO/U, AMO/U/V/X, ANF/P/R/U/V/X, AOA-E, AHG/J/L/N-P/U/V/X-Z, AJO/U/V/X/Y/F/G/J

Date	Deliveries	Licensed for Service
01.10	VW 1034	
02.10	VW 1035-1037	
03.10	VW 1038-1043, 1047-1055	VW 1034-1038, 1048, 1054, 1055 (**AH**)
04.10		VW 1039-1047, 1049-1053 (**AH**)
09.10	VW 1056-1067	VW 1056-1059, 1062 (**AH**)
10.10	VW 1068-1072	VW 1060, 1061, 1063-1072 (**AH**)
05.11	VW 1175-1184	
06.11	VW 1185-1192	VW 1175-1192 (**PA**)
07.11	VW 1193-1195, 1197	
08.11	VW 1196, 1198-1204	VW 1193-1195 (**PA**)
09.11		VW 1196-1204 (**PA**)
11.11	VW 1205-1216	VW 1205-1216 (**PV**)
03.12	VW 1243-1256, 1258-1262	
04.12	VW 1257, 1263-1271	VW 1243-1256, 1258-1262, 1264, 1265, 1267, 1269, 1271 (**HT**)
05.12	VW 1272-1280	VW 1257, 1263, 1266, 1270, 1272-1276 (**HT**)
06.12	VW 1291-1300	VW 1277-1289 (**HT**)
07.12	VW 1301-1304	VW 1300-1304 (**HT**)
08.12	VW 1305, 1306	VW 1305 (**HT**)
09.12		VW 1290, 1293, 1295-1300, 1306 (**HT**)
10.12	VW 1365, 1372, 1374, 1375, 1377-1379, VWH 1360-1364	VW 1292 (**HT**)
11.12	VW 1366-1371, 1373, 1376, 1380-1388	VW 1365-1384, 1386 (**HT**) VWH 1360-1364 (**HT**)
12.12	VW 1393-1397	VW 1385, 1387 (**HT**)
01.13	VW 1389-1392, 1398-1404 VWH 1408-1411, 1414, 1416-1419	VW 1388-1390 (**HT**)
02.13	VW 1405, 1406, VWH 1412, 1415	VW 1391, 1392 (**HT**), VW 1393-1404 (**AC**) VWH 1408-1411, 1414, 1416-1419 (**AC**)
03.13	VW 1407, 1468, VWH 1413	VW 1405, VWH 1412, 1413 (**AC**)
04.13		VW 1406, 1407 (**AC**), VW 1468 (**HT**)
05.14	VWH 2001, 2002, 2004, 2005, 2007, 2010, 2011	
06.14	VWH 2003, 2006, 2008, 2009, 2012-2021	VWH 2001 (**PA**)
07.14	VWH 2022, 2023	VWH 2022 (**PA**)
08.14		VWH 2023 (**PA**)
10.14	VWH 2024-2029	
11.14	VWH 2029-2045	VWH 2024-2029, 2032, 2036-2041 (**PB**)
12.14	VWH 2046-2052, 2055, 2056	VWH 2030, 2031, 2033-2035, 2043-2045 (**PB**)
01.15	VWH 2050, 2053, 2054, 2057-2060	VWH 2042, 2046-2048, 2051, 2053-2056 (**PB**)
02.15	VWH 2061	VWH 2049, 2052, 2058-2060 (**PB**)
03.15		VWH 2061 (**PB**)
04.15		VWH 2050, 2057 (**PB**)
05.15	VWH 2088-2091, 2093-2096, 2098, 2100-2104, 2106, 2108-2119, 2121	
06.15	VWH 2092, 2097, 2099, 2105, 2107, 2120	VWH 2091, 2093, 2095, 2096, 2102, 2106 (**AC**)
07.15		VWH 2088, 2089, 2100, 2104, 2109, 2111, 2113, 2118 (**AC**)
08.15		VWH 2090, 2092, 2098, 2101, 2103, 2105, 2107, 2108, 2110, 2112, 2114-2117, 2119 (**AC**)
10.15	VWH 2123, 2124, 2126-2130, 2133, 2139	VWH 2094, 2097, 2099, 2121, 2123, 2124, 2126-2130, 2133, 2139 (**WJ**)
11.15	VWH 2122, 2125, 2131, 2132, 2134-2138, 2140-2144	VWH 2122, 2131-2137, 2140 (**WJ**)
12.15		VWH 2125, 2138, 2141-2144 (**WJ**)

Date	Deliveries	Licensed for Service
06.16	VWH 2167, 2214-2216	
07.16	VWH 2213, 2222	VWH 2213, 2222 (**HD**)
08.16	VWH 2168-2193, 2217-2221	VWH 2214-2219, 2221, 2224 (**HD**)
09.16	VWH 2194, 2199, 2200, 2202-2212, 2230, 2232	VWH 2167-2186 (**UX**) VWH 2187-2193, 2201, 2220, 2223 (**HD**)
10.16	VWH 2195-2198, 2225-2229, 2231, 2233-2243	VWH 2194, 2199, 2200, 2202, 2203, 2205, 2207, 2209-2212 (**HD**)
11.16		VWH 2204, 2206, 2208, 2226, 2227, 2229-2238, 2240, 2241 (**HD**)
12.16		VWH 2195, 2228, 2239, 2242, 2243 (**HD**)
01.17		VWH 2196, 2197 (**HD**)
04.17	VWH 2266-2275, 2277, 2279, 2288, 2305-2314	
05.17	VWH 2276, 2278, 2280, 2281, 2284, 2285, 2287, 2289, 2292, 2297, 2311, 2315, 2321	VWH 2267, 2270 (**PA**)
06.17	VWH 2282, 2283, 2286, 2290, 2293-2296, 2298-2304, 2316-2320, 2322-2326, 2328	VWH 2266, 2268, 2269, 2271-2284 (**PA**), VWH 2307, 2308, 2313, 2314 (**AC**)
07.17	VWH 2291, 2327, 2329, 2339	VWH 2285, 2286, 2290, 2293, 2296 (**PV**), VWH 2309, 2315, 2317 (**AC**)
08.17	VWH 2330-2338, 2340-2344	VWH 2292, 2295, 2297, 2299, 2302 (**PV**)
09.17	VWH 2345-2349, 2351-2358, 2360, 2361, 2364-2371, 2373-2383	VWH 2288, 2291, 2298, 2300, 2301, 2303-2305 (**PV**), VWH 2289, 2311, 2318-2320, 2322, 2323, 2326-2329, 2331, 2332, 2343, 2341 (**UX**), VWH 2306, 2310, 2312, 2316, 2321, 2324 (**AC**)
10.17	VWH 2350, 2359, 2362, 2363, 2372	VWH 2345-2349, 2351-2353, 2355-2362 (**UX**), VWH 2325, 2333, 2335, 2339, 2372 (**AC**), VWH 2336, 2337 (**PA**)
11.17	VWH 2382, 2389-2391, 2413, 2415, 2417	VWH 2294 (**PA**), VWH 2350, 2362, 2363 (**UX**), VWH 2330, 2334, 2338, 2340, 2342-2344, 2364-2371, 2374 (**AC**)
12.17	VWH 2383-2388, 2392, 2393, 2395-2408, 2410-2412, 2414, 2416, 2418-2431	VWH 2287 (**PA**), VWH 2354 (**UX**), VWH 2379-2381 (**AC**)
01.18	VWH 2394	VWH 2373, 2375-2378, 2382, 2383, 2385-2393, 2395-2398, 2414, 2417-2419 (**AC**), VWH 2287 (**PV**), VWH 2394, 2413 (**PA**)
02.18	VWH 2409, 2432	VWH 2399, 2401-2408, 2410, 2411, 2420-2424, 2426 (**AC**)
03.18		VWH 2412, 2416 (**AC**)
04.18		VWH 2400, 2409, 2425, 2427-2429, 2431, 2432 (**AC**), VWH 2430 (**PA**)
05.18	VMH 2455-2462	

Acquired from First London, 22.06.13
VW 1752-1782, 1817-1894   ex-First London VN 37773-37803, 37865-37942

Disposals
11.17	VW 1846-1848, 1851
01.18	VW 1849, 1850
02.18	VW 1852-1894
03.18	VW 1842, 1843
05.18	VW 1844, 1845

Arriva London

HV 1-152, 201-412, VLW 901-910

The hybrid revolution was ushered in at the end of the first decade of the 21st century with no small help from central government, owing to the tremendous cost of development.

After experience with all-Wrightbus double-decker HEV 1 new in 2007, Arriva ordered examples of the first two competing models out of the gate. As well as five more VDL-derived Wrightbus integrals (to be HWs), there were six of Volvo's new B5LH double-decker, also with Wrightbus Gemini 2 bodywork. To defray the costs of evaluating them, TfL would reimburse the operators.

HV 1-6 were built by the autumn of 2008 and one of them appeared at Euro Bus Expo

held on 4-6 November; in fact an example of each of the current evaluation models from Alexander Dennis, Optare and Wrightbus were present. Both HWs and HVs were earmarked to operate on the 141, where HEV 1 had run intermittently before it was decided to replace that bus's underpowered 1.9-litre Vauxhall Vectra engine with a 2.4-litre Ford one normally found under a Transit van's bonnet. The HVs' auxiliary powerplant was a bit more assertive, being a 5-litre Volvo D5 engine; capacity was H39/21D and overall length 10.34m with a pronounced rear overhang.

HV 2, carrying no numberplate or identification, was displayed at the Lord Mayor's Show on 2 December 2008, and delivery tentatively began in February 2009 via Volvo's premises in Brimsdown. Testing was carried out by Volvo during February and March before the vehicles were formally released to Arriva London North. 58-registrations had been booked for the sextet but were subsequently voided and the buses licensed with 09-marks.

The HWs beat the HVs into service, the Volvos still carrying out familiarisation runs up and down the 141 by that time (mid-April), but in June all six HVs were taken into stock at Arriva and were ready to go. Entry into service was the privilege of HV 2 on 10 June, HVs 3-6 following over the next three days. Saturday working of both HVs and HWs on the 141 commenced on 20 June, and HEV 1 moved on after that, its work done. An official launch ceremony at Alexandra Palace on 7 July starred HVs 3 and 4, and from 2 August Sunday working commenced.

HV 1 went back to Sweden for modifications, returning on 21 July with the intention being for the others to follow one by one.

Below: **On 10 October 2010 one of the pioneering six Volvo B5LHs, HV 3 (LJ09 KOU) is heading south along New North Road in Hoxton.**
Terry Wong Min

HV 3 was sent on loan to Lothian between 25 January and 1 February 2010. In March HVs 3 and 4 were obliged to swap registrations when a mismatch between their identities and chassis numbers was discovered.

A £30m Green Bus fund announced in December 2009 awarded TfL forty-six of the over 300 buses to be ordered, and on 29 March it was announced that twenty of them would be B5LHs for Arriva. The priority for hybrids was identified early, that is to say, addressing pollution issues on a range of identified London corridors. In Arriva London North's case, one of these was the Hertford Road, so HVs 7-26 were to be allocated to Tottenham for the 76 as well as part of the 149 (once otherwise converted from artic to double-deck with DWs) and 243; indeed, only these routes were to be carried on their blinds. The first six HVs would join them after further modifications requiring a trip to Sweden.

HVs 7-26 started to arrive in mid-November and type training commenced at Tottenham, route 76 drivers being first. After acceptance at Volvo's Brimsdown facility, deliveries went to Stamford Hill where ticket machines and Oyster equipment were installed. Remedial recertification work carried out at Brimsdown delayed the HVs' entry into service, but even before that, twenty more were ordered alongside 37 DWs for the prestige task of restoring the 73 to double-deck operation from artics.

17 January saw the HVs' debut on the 76 and all were in service at Tottenham by February. A test was applied to HVs 7 and 9 on 20 January at Enfield whereby both were heated in the paint booth to 41° without detriment to the mechanicals or paintwork. HVs 1-3 duly moved from Wood Green to Tottenham late in February, followed on 3 March by HVs 5 and 6.

Above: **The cheerful leaves of the hybrid livery had unfortunately been toned down by the time Tottenham's HVs for the 76 came into being. Seen at St Paul's Cathedral on 3 July 2011, all that HV 19 (LJ60 AWN) can muster is a single tiny leaf hanging off the 'y' of its redesigned hybrid logo.** *Author*

Left: **Now transferred from Wood Green to Tottenham to join its newer siblings, HV 6 (LJ09 KOW) turns round at Waterloo on 24 September 2011.** *Author*

Right: **The rear aspect of the production Wright-bodied B5LH was unmistakably goofy, with its short wheelbase and long rear overhang, but all of it was contained within the same footprint as a comparable diesel bus, so no clearance troubles were encountered. Still, Arriva's choice of positioning of some of the traditional accoutrements leaves much to be desired by London Transport's standards; the legal lettering is where the fleetnumber's supposed to be, the posted weight is carried underneath that rather than along the skirt, and there's a roundel crammed into the only space left on the side where there's room for one!** *Author*

Below: **The 76's HVs turned out on the 149 before long, this appearance at London Bridge on 28 July 2012 being courtesy of HV 14 (LJ60 AXG).** *Author*

Appearances on anything other than the 76 were to prove rarer than first envisaged, the 149 not seeing one until 16 August. As they entered service, the HVs gained the new, rather tamed hybrid logos and TfL roundel combination.

The 73's batch commenced delivery on 20 June in advance of the 3 September changeover date and all but HV 39 were in stock prior to Wrightbus's summer holiday shutdown. Upon its conversion from MAL, the 73 would operate from Stamford Hill.

HV 39 duly arrived on 20 August and the 73 was converted on 3 September. Not all the DWs were in stock yet, so VLWs had to help out; the N73 also assumed double-deck operation. One new route for the HVs from the outset was the 253 out of Stamford Hill.

Confidence in the B5LH was now high enough for Volvo to announce in October that the 76's fleet was offering a 37% fuel saving over comparable diesel buses.

The two routes' worth of HVs settled down, very little troubling them over the rest of 2011 and into 2012. For the moment, the impetus in terms of hybrid technology had passed to the New Bus for London, a.k.a. the Borismaster; the first eight entered service on Arriva London North's own 38 over the spring of 2012 and the expected production order would be set to colonise the City and West End. Even so, in May an order was

Right: **HV 61 (LJ62 BZH) was one of the batch that installed 100% hybrid operation on the 73 and let its DWs depart for VLW replacement. On 22 December 2012 it is seen about to make the left turn into Victoria bus station, where it will terminate.** *Author*

placed for a whopping 75 HVs alongside forty more DWs. Thirty-seven of them would be added to Stamford Hill to join HVs 27-46 on the 73 and thereby convert it to full hybrid operation, and the others would be against the 29's retention on tender, displacing the DWs that had already taken it over from artics. Arriva was thus about to have over a hundred hybrids in service, and in September it got even better for the HV class when the order was increased by ten.

HVs 47-81 began arriving on 5 November and went into service from 5 December, displacing DWs to ease DLAs off the 41 and 243. HV 40 was loaned to Arriva Southern Counties on 14 and 15 January 2013 to carry

Below: **On 2 June 2013 HV 73 (LJ62 BVP) has made that left turn and is about to take its place in the congested queue at Victoria bus station.** *Author*

Above: **Warren Street has been through a host of changes in recent years, and the advent of HVs on the 29 was no different. On 7 July 2013 Wood Green's HV 102 (LJ13 FBY) heads north.** *Author*

out route tests from Maidstone in anticipation of the delivery of similar vehicles. All were in service by February 2013, two late stragglers drawing the process out.

The 29's contract applied from 12 January but its assigned new fleet (HVs 84-131, with HVs 82 and 83 diverted to top up the 73) wasn't due till April, by which time 13-registrations would be in force. HV 55 was sent to Wood Green between 12 March and 16 April to serve as a trainer. As it turned out, the highest-numbered batch of HVs were delivered first and two of them kicked off the new era on the 29 (and N29) on 29 April. They lost no time wandering to the 144 at Wood Green, and then the 221. HV 106, however, caught fire while on test around Ballymena on 7 June and was written off before it even got to the mainland. A replacement was commissioned under warranty.

And still there were more HVs to come, when in June an order for 21 was placed against the award (and retention) of the 319 based on new buses.

Left: **At the Wood Green end of the 29 (the roads onward to Palmers Green having been transferred to the 141 when artics took over the 29), HV 124 (LJ13 FAU) gets ready to head south on 2 June 2013.** *Author*

Right: **Stamford Hill's HVs liked to wander to the 67, and at Aldgate on 7 July 2013 HV 55 (LJ62 BNL) is setting off.** *Author*

Right: **The 149 was the third choice for HVs after the 76 and 243, and at a considerably changed Edmonton on 2 June 2013 we see HV 23 (LJ60 AWU).** *Author*

Right: **Completing this page's trio of oddments is the Wood Green version, which took HVs off the 29 to the 144. HV 94 (LJ13 FCP) is doing just that when captured at Turnpike Lane on 5 April 2014.** *Author*

August 2013 saw the first HV into an all-over advert livery; this was Stamford Hill's HV 38 for the Gap and it lasted till October.

Now that the 29 was complete (its HVs, bar one, having gone into service in July), it was time to prepare Brixton, and the second HV 106 was delivered there on 10 November for that purpose. Spanning Wright's Christmas shutdown, five were shipped to Heysham by the end of December and the rest followed in January. However, it was to be the 59 that hosted them; as with the 87 and 88 at London General, the hybrids were diverted to central London services to address an increasing perception of pollution problems. Once service entry began on 27 January, they did see service on their intended 319, but only as second choice to the 59. HV 106 entered service at Wood Green on the same day.

Above: **The replacement HV 106 (LT63 UKJ) is seen arriving at Trafalgar Square on 18 January 2015.** *Author*

Left: **Meant for the 319, the HVs into Brixton congregated on the 59 instead. On 27 February 2015 HV 143 (LT63 UJD) is plying south through Holborn.** *Author*

Left: **On 18 January 2015 Brixton has put out HV 140 (LT63 UJX) at least on the 319, and it is caught at Clapham Junction heading north.** *Author*

Hybrids may have been the future of London's buses (and none more so than the Borismaster, which was now entering service in large numbers), but Volvo was still trying one last time with the diesel bus, producing the B5TL. Three came to London for evaluation by London companies, and BF63 HDE was Arriva's representative, appearing in March as VGD 1 (see page 186).

The rest of 2014 was settled to the point of near non-activity for Arriva's HV class; HVs 25 and 26 moved from Tottenham to Stamford Hill in March and HV 25 then wore an ad for the Gap between August and November. The 76's HVs at Tottenham were shifted to the 149 and 243 after 8 November until blinds incorporating the new Tottenham Hale terminus of the 76 were printed; that was done by 18 November and the HVs returned.

2014 had already seen the heavily-trafficked 38 within Arriva go over to LT operation and 2015 began with the same fate for the 137 at Brixton; an appearance by HV 147 on 22 December was the only time an HV had strayed off the 59 or 319, and they never visited the 109 or 159. The 73 was then earmarked for Borismasters, setting up a great cascade of HVs. When this commenced on 14 May, the 73's fleet was divided, HVs 25-56 staying at Stamford Hill to convert the 253 from VLW operation, and the rest moving to the 141 to strike up a new allocation for the class at Palmers Green. This commenced on 15 June after the first two of the intended batch had carried out type training. Eleven of the 141's 29 workings were outstationed to Wood Green (though on Palmers Green numbers, should they deign to display any), and vehicles were pooled. New blinds printed for Wood Green at the same time ensured early HV visits to the 184 and W3, though not the 221, and similar equipping of Palmers Green's new HV intake saw appearances on the 102 and 329.

In May or thereabouts Tottenham's HV 7 was given an in-house advert extolling the virtues of 'green' buses and boasting the fact that 1,200 hybrids were now in service.

Left: **Borismasters began to edge the HVs off the 73 on 14 May, and on the following morning we see LT 464 (LTZ 1464) pulling past HV 77 (LJ62 BFZ) at Euston Square station.** *Author*

Left: **HV 42 (LJ11 EFN) stayed put at Stamford Hill after the Borismasters came and switched its allegiance to the 253 instead. It is seen heading uphill from Holloway on 6 August 2015. Before long the 253 would assume LT operation as well.** *Author*

Left: **Just as the last leaf-adorned HVs were going through repaint, HV 7 (LJ60 AWY) received an all-over ad that brought the leaves back. On 22 May 2015 it is seen at Old Street.** *Author*

Right: **HV 62 (LJ62 BZR) was transferred to Palmers Green and took up on the 141, being seen in service on that route at London Bridge on 19 December 2015. Eleven of the 29 workings on the 141 were actually outstationed to Wood Green, but you'd never know it, as both Arriva London North garages have slacked off lately on displaying running numbers.** *Author*

The next LT route at Arriva was to be the 149, removing it from HV consideration between 13 October and the end of that month. It seemed that where hybrids had been flavour of the month in 2013 and 2014, it was now the turn of the Borismaster, which chased the HVs off their routes one by one. Between 22 March and 28 April 2016 the 59 at Brixton was taken over by LTs, allowing its HVs to concentrate on the 319 as originally intended. Borismasters were also pencilled in for the 253 during the year, and in June plans were made to convert the 76, lost to Go-Ahead in 2017 (and which would in turn supply Brixton with HVs to regain the 333 and share the 133 with HA-class Enviro400City vehicles ordered in June). But Borismaster production was winding down, a new Mayor having declined to continue taking the type, and the Volvo B5LH came back into the ascendancy. In July 25 were ordered against the winning back of the 259, and in the autumn that

Below: **One of Wood Green's own B5LHs, HV 103 (LJ13 FBZ) offers a perfect offside shot through the 141's diversion away from the lower end of Bishopsgate on 19 December 2015.** *Author*

order was boosted to a hefty 123 to take in concurrent wins or retentions of the 2, 19, 242 and 249. These would be to the new Gemini 3 redesign and, in accordance with current Arriva practice, leap up to start a new block of fleetnumbers as HVs 201-323.

Palmers Green's HV 64 was selected for special treatment evoking a much older and much-loved London fixture; to this end, in July it assumed not only the silver colour of long-departed Routemaster RM 664, but also its registration, which had been perching on DW 64 for a decade. It was done in aid of Arriva's charitable exercise on behalf of the company's payroll, with 1,000 employees being commemorated on the signwriting.

Below: **The new Silver Lady, HV 64 (WLT 664, ex-LJ62 BAO), takes its gleaming colour scheme through Wood Green as dusk seeps in on 27 August 2017. This was actually during its second stint at Palmers Green, the bus having spent a long period at Brixton on the 50.** *Author*

In July two HVs received ads; HV 141 for Zoopla and HV 146 for U-Switch. HV 7 had done over a year in its green wrap and in August reverted to red.

Route 253 was next for LT conversion and this got started in October, displacing Stamford Hill's last HVs. Three topped up the 141, while six into Tottenham (plus five transfers from Wood Green) allowed the conversion of the 67 to HV operation. The most significant HV transfers, however, were south of the river to convert Brixton's 50, thereby turning that garage over to 100% hybrid operation. They were part of a complicated shuffle by which, through displacing DWs to Norwood, the latter garage could release

enough T-class Enviro400s to Thornton Heath to make possible the acquisition of the 157 from Abellio on 2 December.

Brixton's 100% hybrid status didn't last, as on 21 January 2017 DWs had to be transferred back in from Norwood when the 333 was regained; the 76's handover to London General was postponed to 25 March, thus keeping its HVs for two more months. However, the move of the 133 from Norwood to Brixton on 21 January ensured the appearance of HVs from the outset.

Above: **The Gemini 3 redesign duly came to Arriva fleets in 2017 in the person of 123 Volvo B5LHs continuing the HV class, or rather causing it to leap to a new numbering block starting at 201 rather than the more logical progression. On 2 February Tottenham began running its new buses in early in advance of the 259's return on 28 February, and on the 13th HV 204 (LK66 HCJ) is seen at Wood Green on the 243.** *Author*

The 'Fugly' HVs began arriving in January 2017 and on 2 February two were noted on the 243 out of Tottenham; these were from the 25-strong batch intended for the 259 from 28 February. Clapton's batch (HV 226-248) for the 242 from 25 February commenced entering service on the 20th, and on 8 March the 2 at Norwood commenced conversion from VLA operation. This garage's batch, including the 249's complement when it was taken over on 1 April, comprised HVs 294-323. When Tottenham took over the 19 on 1 April it received HVs 249-279, although DWs were in evidence from the outset here.

Right: **Clapton's HV 232 (LK66 GBO) comes round the corner from Amherst Road past Hackney Central Station on 21 March 2017. The Narroway has been pedestrianised in the interim, resulting in this long and cumbersome diversion.** *Author*

Left: **Only days into service, Clapton's HV 230 (LK66 GBE) is already sporting battle damage that has needed to be taped up when sighted at Liverpool Street on 3 March 2017.** *Author*

Left: **On Sunday 26 March 2017, the day after the 259 went back to Arriva London North, Tottenham's HV 217 (LK66 HDE) heads south past Seven Sisters station.** *Author*

Left: **HV 50 (LJ62 BHY) out of Tottenham was paying a visit to the 243 when caught at Seven Sisters on 26 March 2017.** *Author*

Above: **The 2 was mostly HV-operated by the time Norwood's HV 311 (LK17 AHO) was sighted at Brixton on 26 March 2017. As well as the 249 gained on 1 May, the new buses inevitably wandered to the 417.** *Author*

Right: **A diversion of the 29 away from the southern end of Charing Cross Road has brought Wood Green's HV 124 (LJ13 FAU) past the morning photo pitch at Trafalgar Square on 26 March 2017.** *Author*

In March Zoopla-liveried HV 141 was returned to red and HV 146 regained red in April (ex-uSwitch). During April HV 64 moved from Wood Green to Brixton and was put out on the 50 for the most part.

Two important Arriva London North routes were retained when two separate tranches were announced; these were the 341 in February and the 243 in March, for commencement dates later in 2017. In April 56 more HVs were ordered to cover them both, comprising HVs 324-379.

During July two of the 60-reg HVs became the first of their class to go through the

Above: **On 3 April 2017, two days after Arriva London North's takeover of the 19, Tottenham's brand new HV 264 (LK66 GFV) pauses just south of Highbury Corner.** *Author*

Left: **HV 311 (LK17 AHO) out of Norwood garage sets off from Clapham Common station on 3 April 2017.** *Author*

refurbishment process. On 8 August HV 64 resumed service from Palmers Green, returning to the 141. August was also the month in which the HVs for the 243 and 341 started arriving.

Three HVs were adorned with adverts in July; HV 101 for Go North Wales and HV 128 for the London Metropolitan University were routine, but HV 244 was the first Fugly, and its green scheme for Avocado improved its lines considerably.

On 2 September HVs 73-89 were transferred from Wood Green to Palmers Green now that extra space was available.

In the autumn the award of the 468 back to Arriva London South was announced, to take effect in the New Year, and September saw an order placed for 33 more HVs. The HV 324-

Left: **For all the buses that pass through it, Finsbury Park is a surprisingly difficult place to photograph; the bus station is at the wrong angle for any time of day and the sliver of sunshine between the shadows at late afternoon will confound more times than it will produce success. However, the traffic has parted (just about) for North Wales-liveried HV 101 (LJ13 FDC) of Wood Green on 27 August 2017.** *Author*

379 batch started entering service on the 341 on 11 September, with the 243 following suit as deliveries picked up. To address visibility problems from the outside the blind boxes were brought closer to the window glass.

One big surprise in September brought Arriva London its first Volvo B9TLs; despite taking to the hybrid B5LH with gusto, the diesel version had been entirely ignored in favour of VDL and ADL products. Taking the numbers VLW 901-910, therefore, were ten of the former Tower Transit VNs of 61-registration recently displaced from the

295. They were intended for the 123, whose 03-reg VLAs had never managed to conquer the noise problems common to the Volvo B7TL type and were now approaching sale age anyway. On 4 October the 67 (with HV 38-56) was formally transferred from Tottenham to Stamford Hill, where its drivers hailed from.

A glut of adverts in October turned Avocado HV 244 into a Google Pixel 2 with the white of this scheme over the front as well; it was joined by HVs 245-248 from the 242's batch and HV 270-277 from the 19.

Below: **The 56 Wrightbus Gemini 3-bodied B5LHs delivered in the last quarter of 2017 for the 243 and 341 are represented at Waterloo by Tottenham's HV 335 (LF67 EUB) on 6 December. With this batch, the blinds are easier to see and there has also been some compromise with the 341's destination, following on from TfL's bewildering hang-up against showing shop names.** *Author*

Above: **Tower Transit's shortsightedness when it came to retaining newer vehicles as competitive tools was Arriva's gain, ten of its outgoing VNs passing via Ensign to lower the age quotient on the 123. Seeing off an exhausted VLA at Tottenham Hale on 4 January 2018 is VLW 903 (BN61 MXM), formerly known as VN 37965 from the 266's batch and new, of course, to First London.** *Author*

At the same time HV 265 was treated to an ad for Zillertal in Austria. All these adverts lasted until January.

With just four of the original VLW class left in stock at the turn of the year, the B9TL variant commenced service on the 123 on 2 January 2018, moving with the route to Edmonton. On the 6th 27 of the 38 workings on Tottenham's 149 were outstationed to Edmonton, prompting sizeable numbers of HVs to begin turning out alongside the scheduled Borismasters. This lasted until 17 March.

HV 380-412, the 468's complement from 31 March 2018, started delivery in January and were stockpiled at Norwood, the route's

Right: **HVs were also common on the 123 by the turn of 2018. Tottenham's HV 324 (LJ17 WOH) is espied setting off from Wood Green on 25 February.** *Author*

intended operator, although some of them were pressed into service on rail replacement work on 24 February, by which time they had been licensed, all but the late-arriving last two retaining their 67-registrations. When they did reach the 468, they were inevitably pooled with the earlier examples from the 2 and 249, and vice versa.

During February HVs 244 and 275 lost their adverts, but HV 235 donned one for

the Hopper ticket variant of the Oyster card, followed in March by HV 355. March also saw HV 35 adorned with a Green Bus advert, and Michael Kors ads appeared on four HVs (229, 238, 255 and 259). HV 128 wore an advert for London Metropolitan University but lost it in April.

It had been a long time since a re-registration with a Routemaster mark, the once-popular craze having tailed off in recent years, but in May 2018 HV 376 was re-registered WLT 676.

A routine change with a fairly predictable consequence was Palmers Green's takeover of the 340 from Garston on 9 June. From the second day HVs could be seen in strength despite the acquisition of the route's dedicated ten SW-class Streetdecks.

Left: **A fortuitous bit of roadworks in the Victoria one-way system on 3 June 2018 has channelled southbound buses into perfect nearside positions, and just one such capture that morning is of Norwood's HV 307 (LK17 AHE) on its regular route 2 work.** *Author*

Left: **A lucky afternoon on 8 July 2018 caught silver HV 64 (WLT 664, ex-LJ62 BAO) straying off its normal 141 onto the 329. It is setting off from Turnpike Lane.** *Author*

Left: **Dogged determination rather than luck brought in this picture of HV 76 (LJ62 BWP) on the 340 on the outskirts of Edgware on 8 July. In fact, three of this Sunday's complement out of Palmers Green were HVs. The 340's new operating garage is a colossal distance away, but then again, so was Garston.** *Author*

Above: **To round off Arriva's participation in this account of the first ten years of Volvo's B9TL and B5LH is a shot of recently re-registered HV 376 (WLT 676, ex-LF67 EVN) on 8 July 2018, crossing Balls Pond Road on its way to Newington Green and points north. The marvellous London Vehicle Finder must be acknowledged here, as it enabled this bus (and others in this book) to be tracked all over town and intercepted at a suitable point.** *Author*

Registrations

HV 1-6	LJ09 KRU, KOE/U/H/V/W
HV 7-26	LJ60 AWY/Z, AXA-D/F/G, AWF-H/M-P/R/U/V, JGY/Z
HV 27-46	LJ11 EFT-Z, EGC/D, EFE-G/K-P/R, EEU
HV 47-81	LJ62 BEO, BGK/X, BHY, BKU/X, BMZ, BNE/L/U, BXD/F, BYT/U, BZH/R/Y, BAO/U, BCU, BND, BPV, BSO, BTO/Y, BVE/P/Y, BWF/P, BFZ, BGZ, BHF, BJK/X
HV 82-131	LJ13 FDD-G/K-P, FCN-P/U/V/X-Z, FDA-C, FBY/Z, FCA/C-G/L/M, FBE-G/K/L/N/O/U/V/X, FAM/O/U, FBA-D, FEO/P/T
HV 106 (ii)	LT63 UKJ *(the original HV 106 was destroyed by fire before being licensed)*
HV 132-152	LT63 UHR, UJO/P/R/S/U-Z, UJD-H/J-N
HV 201-271	LK66 HCF-H/J/L/N-P/U/V/X-Z, HDA/C-H, LJ17 WVF, LK66 HDL/N/O/U, LJ17 WVG, LK66 GAO/U/X, GBE/F/O, LJ17 WVH, LK66 GBV/X-Z, GCF/O/U/V/X-Z, GDA/E/F/J/O/U/V/X-Z, GEJ/U/Y, GFA/E/G/J/O/U/V/X-Z, GGA/E/F/J
HV 272-323	LK17 AFA/E/F/J/N/O/U/V, AKJ/N/O/P/U/X-Z, ALO/U, AMO/U/V/X, AFX-Z, AGO/U/V/X-Z, AHA/C-E/G/J/L/O/P/U/V/X-Z, AJO/U/V/X/Y, AKG
HV 324-333	LJ17 WOH/M/R/U/X/Y, WPA/D/E
HV 334-379	LF67 EUA-E/H/J-P/R/T-Z, EVB-D/W/U/R, EWB, EVX/T, EWA, EVY, EWC/E/G/D/H, EVH/J/G/P/M/N/L/K, EWJ, EVW/U/R, EWB, EVX/T, EWA, EVY, EWE/G/D/H, EVH/J/G/P/M/N/L/K, EWJ
HV 380-410	LC67 AHE-G/J-L/N-P/X/Y, AJU, AHU, AJO, AHV, AJX, AKG/F, AHZ, AJY, AKK, AJV, AKJ/N/P/U, ACU, AKO, ACY/X/Z
HV 411, 412	LF18 AWZ, AWA

Re-registrations

03.10	HV 3 from LJ09 KOU to LJ09 KOH
03.10	HV 4 from LJ09 KOH to LJ09 KOU
07.15	HV 64 from LJ62 BAO to WLT 664
05.18	HV 376 from LF67 EVN to WLT 676

Date	Deliveries	Licensed for Service
06.09	HV 1-6	HV 1-6 (**WN**)
10.10	HV 8, 12	
11.10	HV 7	
12.10	HV 9-11, 13-23	
01.11	HV 24, 25	HV 7-23 (**AR**)
02.11	HV 26	HV 24-26 (**AR**)
06.11	HV 27-38, 40-42	
07.11	HV 43-46	
08.11	HV 39	
09.11		HV 27-46 (**SF**)
11.12	HV 47-52, 54-64, 66, 67, 70	
12.12	HV 53, 68, 69, 71, 72, 74, 75	HV 47-64, 66-72, 74, 75 (**SF**)
01.13	HV 73, 77-81	HV 73, 77-81 (**SF**)
02.13	HV 65, 76	HV 65, 76 (**SF**)
04.13	HV 122-135, 127-130	HV 122-135, 127-130 (**WN**)
05.13	HV 82-95, 97, 114, 115, 126, 131	HV 126, 131 (**WN**)
06.13	HV 96, 98-105, 107-112, 118-120	HV 82, 83 (**SF**), HV 84-105, 107-112, 114-120 (**WN**)
07.13	HV 113, 121	HV 113, 121 (**WN**)
11.13	HV 106(ii)	
01.14	HV 132-145	HV 106(ii) (**WN**), HV 132-140 (**BN**)
02.14	HV 146-151	HV 141-145, 147-150 (**BN**)
03.14	HV 152	HV 146, 151, 152 (**BN**)
01.17	HV 205, 206, 209, 211-215, 218, 219, 223-225, 227, 230, 249-251	HV 201, 202, 204, 206 (**AR**)
02.17	HV 216, 217, 222, 228, 229, 231, 232, 234-245, 248, 252-262, 264, 266, 267, 270, 281, 282, 284-286, 288, 295-306, 309, 311	HV 203, 205, 207, 208, 210, 212-215, 217-219 (**AR**), HV 227, 228, 230-232, 235, 237 (**CT**)
03.17	HV 220, 221, 233, 246, 247, 263, 265, 268, 269, 271-277, 279, 280, 283, 287, 289, 290, 292-294, 307, 310, 312-321	HV 209, 211, 216, 220, 222-225, 249-271, 273, 274, 276, 277 (**AR**), HV 229, 234, 242, 248 (**CT**) HV 280-288, 295-311, 313, 317 (**N**)
04.17	HV 226, 278, 291, 308, 322, 323	HV 233, 236, 238, 239, 243, 245, 246 (**CT**) HV 221, 272, 275, 278, 279 (**AR**) HV 289, 290, 292-294, 314, 316, 318, 319 (**N**)
05.17		HV 226, 240, 247 (**CT**), HV 291, 312, 321, 322 (**N**)
08.17	HV 324-333	
09.17	HV 335-341, 346, 347, 349-352, 354-362, 374, 371-375	HV 324-334, 336 (**AR**)
10.17	HV 348, 363, 365-369, 376-379	HV 335, 337-343, 345, 347 (**AR**)
11.17	HV 353	HV 346, 348-350, 352, 354-358, 363, 369, 371, 373, 376, 377, 379 (**AR**)
12.17		HV 360, 362, 364-368, 370, 374, 375, 378 (**AR**)
01.18	HV 380, 381, 383-393, 395, 396, 398, 399, 402, 405, 406 408, 410	HV 351, 359, 361 (**AR**)
02.18	HV 382, 394, 397, 400, 401, 403, 404, 407, 409	HV 383, 384, 388, 393, 394, 396, 399-405, 407, 409 (**N**)

Acquired from Ensign, 09.17 (into service 01.18)
VLW 901-910 ex-Tower Transit VN 37975, 37963, 37965, 37967, 37969, 37970, 37973, 37972, 37971, 37976

Stagecoach

13001-13032, 13061-13102

Below: **Stagecoach Selkent's first Volvos since the Olympian comprised 32 Gemini 3-bodied B5LHs; rather than the 54 and 75 for which they were ordered, they were allocated to the 53 from Plumstead. On 20 November 2014 13020 (BJ14 KSY) turns left onto Westminster Bridge.** *Author*

Resolutely wedded to the Dennis Trident (and not surprisingly, since its parent had been instrumental in pulling the manufacturer out of financial disaster), Stagecoach in London had ignored the Volvo B7TL and B9TL alike to standardise on the Enviro400. But in 2013 a set of tendering wins for Selkent, encompassing first the 96 and 472 out of Plumstead and then the 54 and 75 (which would be returning to Catford after five years with Metrobus) added a Volvo B5LH component for the first time.

To be numbered 13001-13032, thirty-two Wrightbus Gemini 3-bodied Volvo B5LHs would also herald a rare foray into

Wrightbus bodywork for Stagecoach, again invested heavily in the Alexander Dennis body as well as its chassis. It was thought at the time that the new B5LHs would furnish the 54 and 75, and the award of the 205 at the end of 2013 prompted a follow-on order for another thirty, but a decision was made at the start of 2014 to take thirty more E40Hs for the 205 instead and indeed send 13001-13032 to Plumstead, with the intention to displace older Scanias and Tridents.

They started arriving in April 2014 and entered service beginning on the 28th, first on school route 602 and then the 122. Their main allocation was to be to the 53, which first saw

Left: **Plumstead's 13010 (BN14 VZD) shows off the rear view of the redesign, with its awkward wraparound panels, at the 53's first southbound stop in Whitehall on 21 August 2014.** *Author*

a Volvo on 1 May, and the first six displaced an equivalent number of Enviro400s to Rainham for the 372. May's deliveries pushed Tridents out to Catford for an increase to the 136 and all of the B5LHs were in service by June.

The new buses stuck rigidly to their assigned routes 53 and 122, with the first wandering not until 10 August when 13031 visited the 472. August was when the 177's award was announced as staying with

Below: **The lowest-numbered of the batch, 13001 (BU14 EFW), is making a side trip to the 122 when pictured drawing up to Woolwich town centre on 21 August 2014.** *Author*

Above: **Plumstead's 13067 (BF15 KGV) at Woolwich on 10 September 2015 exemplifies the 177's batch of Enviro400 MMC-bodied Volvo B5LHs.** *Author*

Right: **The 177's new buses could also be found on other Plumstead routes, 13061 (BF15 KGK) turning out on the 53 when sighted at the Elephant on 15 August.** *Author*

Stagecoach Selkent on the promise of new hybrid buses, and again the choice was a surprise when an order for 22 Volvo B5LHs was placed, this time with Alexander Dennis Enviro400 MMC bodywork. To be numbered 13061-13082, they followed on from a batch for Stagecoach in Dundee.

Delivery commenced on 28 May, first to Alexander Dennis's premises in Harlow and then to storage at West Ham. 15 June saw the first ones go into service on the 177 out of Plumstead, enabling the release of Scanias across the river. Unlike their Wrightbus-bodied predecessors, these were

Left: The '122' was also treated to appearances by the 177's new motors, and on a sunny 8 January 2016 we see Plumstead's 13075 (BJ15 TVZ) coming up to the Crystal Palace terminus of the 122. *Author*

quicker to stray off the 177, soon racking up appearances on the 51, 53 and 122. Four of them plus two from the earlier batch were part of Stagecoach's contingent at Silverstone in the first weekend of July. The 22nd of the newest batch (to have been 13082) was effectively swapped for another E40H, 12364.

Late in 2015 the 47 was won on tender for a new contract with its incumbent Catford garage, and 21 more Enviro400 MMC-bodied Volvo B5LHs were ordered. These would take numbers 13082-13102. At the same time the 53 was retained in the same manner and a proper dedicated batch of buses was ordered,

Left: The tidying up of the roundabout at St George's Circus permitted considerably better photographs without impediment by street furniture. Plumstead's 13014 (BN14 WAE) comes round on 11 February 2016, the lamp-post shadow showing that it's right at the end of possibility for a shot like this at this period of the year. This bus and its fellows would be displaced from the 53 by the summer, but would continue to feature. *Author*

Above: **Stagecoach London took a second batch of Enviro400MMC bodies on Volvo B5LHs when it came time to upgrade the 47 from 'TA'. Seen opposite Liverpool Street Station on 28 February 2016 is Catford's 13097 (BL65 OYT).** *Author*

comprising MMC E40Hs 12365-12401, which would allow the 53's present batch comprising 13001-13032 to hold in place and send off earlier Enviro400s to East London and replace Tridents.

The 47's batch of B5LHs began staging through ADL Harlow from 16 December and gathered at West Ham. At the same time Plumstead sent 13077 to Catford to get that garage ready for its new intake. 13083 and 13084 entered service on the 47 on 25 January and within a fortnight they were all in place, allowing the route's previous 'TAs' to divide between Bromley and Barking.

Right: **The tidy rear of the MMC is predominantly black, as on Catford's 13091 (BL65 OYK) speeding away from Surrey Quays towards Canada Water on 25 March 2016. The likelihood, unfortunately, is that the black bits that aren't made of smoked glass will be gone over indiscriminately upon repaint sometime in the future.** *Author*

Left: **As with every previous batch of Volvo B5LH into Stagecoach Selkent, the 47's fleet would wander; here at the Elephant's revamped layout southbound on 8 September 2016 is 13085 (BL65 OYD), on the 136's most recent section introduced to back up the 343.**
Author

The 53's Enviro400H MMCs arrived in June and colonised the 53 over the summer to match its contract date of 23 July, and all of a sudden the formerly rigidly-allocated earlier Gemini 3 Volvo B5LHs spread all over Plumstead's routes, covering the 96, 99, 122 and 472, and only the Scania-operated 51 remained exempt.

Below: **This time the 53's buses were those intended for it from the outset, comprising 36 integral Enviro400MMCs, but the previous fleet took a while to get the hint and continued to turn out, as Plumstead's 13023 (BG14 ONS) is doing when drawing up to Westminster on 6 August 2016.**
Author

A local initiative Stagecoach had produced in 2016 was repeated this year with more buses; this was Earth Day, celebrated on 5 June, and the Volvo B5LH representatives into allover green were Plumstead's 13070 (based principally on the 122) and Catford's 13087 from the 47. They lasted quite a bit longer than their 2016 predecessor, returning to red in mid-August.

Quiet has characterised the B5LHs' career at Stagecoach Selkent, but in April 2018 13090 received an all-over advert for Green Bus.

Left: **Serving the shopping complex at East Greenwich on 9 March 2017 is Plumstead's 13027 (BG14 ONW), on a day when the 472 was fielding just about any type the garage could throw at it.** *Author*

Left: **The two Selkent Volvo B5LHs assigned to World Environment duty lingered for a lot longer than 2016's single predecessor did; by 13 August 2017 Catford's 13087 (BL65 OYF), seen on London Bridge, is still green. It was repainted red on the 22nd.** *Author*

Registrations

13001-13032	BU14 EFW-Z, BN14 VZH/J-L, BN14 VZM/O/P/R, WAA/E/J/O, BJ14 KSU/V/X/Y, BG14 ONR/T/S/V/U/X/W, OOA/D, ONZ, OOB/C
13061-13081	BF15 KGK/N/P/U/V/X-Z, KHB/C/D/G/H/J, BJ15 TVZ, TWA, BF15 KHA, BJ15 TWC, BF15 KGJ/O, KHE
13082-13102	BL65 OYA-H/J/K/M-P/R/T-Y

Date	Deliveries	Licensed for Service
04.14	13001-13008, 13011-13016	13001-13008, 13011-13016 (**PD**)
05.14	13009, 13010, 13017-13028, 13030	13009, 13010, 13017-13028, 13030 (**PD**)
06.14	13029, 13031, 13032	13029, 13031, 13032 (**PD**)
05.15	13061, 13062	
06.15	13063-13075, 13077-13079	13061-13075, 13079 (**PD**)
07.15	13076, 13080, 13081	13076-13078, 13080, 13081 (**PD**)
12.15	13082-13091	
01.16	13092-13102	13082-13087, 13097 (**TL**)
02.16		13088-13096, 13098-13102 (**TL**)

London Coaches

VLE 611-620, VXE 721-735

Better known as Arriva presenting London until its latter sale to RATP and trading under 'The Original London Sightseeing Tour' as well as operating a CitySightseeing franchise, what began as London Coaches was retiring its elderly ex-Arriva MCW Metrobuses by the first years of the 21st century and needed something bigger, as well as brand new. After taking Ayats Bravo bodywork on Volvo B7Ls (which combination formed the VLY class), the company thought bigger again and in 2007 ordered ten tri-axle versions of the new Volvo B9TL. These carried East Lancs Visionnaire bodywork to PO49/31F capacity and were numbered VLE 611-620 (LJ07 XEN/O/P/R-W, UDD).

Four years later, fifteen tri-axle B9TLs were taken with 12.35m Visionnaire bodywork (although now labelled Optare, and of capacity PO59/38F), classified VXE 721-735 (YJ11 TVA/C-F/L-P/T/U-X).

Below: **The 2007 incarnation of Showbus on 16 September of that year sees VLE 618 (LJ07 XEV) on display at Duxford.** *Author*

Left: **On 16 June 2013 the enormous bulk of VXE 722 (YJ11 TVC) is seen in Lower Regent Street.** *Author*

Left: **Arriva's touring arm has since been sold to RATP and rebranded as Extrapolitan. Only minor alterations were thus made to the fleet in, as seen on VXE 726 (YJ11 TVK) in Pall Mall on 26 January 2017.** *Author*

Left: **During the spring of 2017, a new and absolutely splendid livery began appearing on Original Tour buses. The fact that it's based on the Union flag is especially eye-opening, given that the owner is French! VXE 731 (YJ11 TVP) rounds Marble Arch on 18 July 2017.** *Author*

For a long time a fixture on the competitive London sightseeing scene, The Big Bus Company had finished with its stalwart ex-London DMSs and gone on to newer (not to mention bigger) things. At first this was Tridents ex-Metrobus, and all formed a DA class denoting 'disabled access'. But in August 2008 ten East Lancs (Optare by the time they were finished) Visionnaire-bodied Volvo B9TLs arrived, numbered DA 201-210

Right: **DA 204 (PF08 URU) crosses Trafalgar Square on the morning of 11 February 2012.** *Author*

Right: **The new Big Bus livery introduced in 2013 was most disappointing by comparison to the original, but at least the key colours of maroon and cream were retained. DA 215 (PN09 EOD) passes along Whitehall on 11 November 2016.** *Author*

and registered PF08 URP/R/S/U-W/X/Z, USB/C. DAs 201-207 were part open-top (PO51/31F) and the other three were fully open-top (O51/31F), with just a front upper deck windscreen. These displaced the long-established Titans, the second generation of ex-London Transport buses, to work across the Big Bus Company's worldwide subsidiaries.

Ten more were ordered for the 2009 season and arrived in March, split between part-open top (DA 211-213) and fully open-top (DA 214-220); the ten were registered PN09 ENY, EOA-F/H/J/K.

Big Bus went even bigger in 2010, taking six 12.35m Volvo B9TLs on three axles. Part-open-topped DAs 321-326, of a whopping PO53/38F capacity, were delivered in March registered PN10 FOC/D/F/H/J/K, but after that the company went Chinese, buying 20 Ankai double-deckers to replace the ex-Hong Kong Metrobuses and Dennis Condors that had latterly bulked out the fleet.

A new livery began appearing in 2013.

Golden Tours

101-124

Golden Tours commenced its own-brand London sightseeing tour operations on 18 June 2011 after a long period hiring coaches. As well as purchasing large numbers of ex-Stagecoach Dennis Tridents, the Wandsworth-based company took its own new part-open-top double-deck buses from the outset, and these were Optare Visionnaire-bodied Volvo B9TLs. New in June 2011, YJ11 OHL/N/O received fleetnumbers 101-103 by the end of the year. Shortly after commencing operations, the company moved to bigger premises near Hayes & Harlington station.

In 2012 Golden Tours won the contract to feed the Harry Potter experience at Warner Brothers Studios in Leavesden, and in May took a Wrightbus Gemini 2-bodied Volvo B9TL numbered 104 (WB12 POT). It was liveried in black with scenes from the movies.

At the end of 2012 Golden Tours ordered nine more Volvo B9TLs, this time with MCV bodywork. Three were closed-top (H45/27F) format and three open-top, and indeed the first of the former arrived in white in December as 105 (BF62 UYN) and went into service on the 27th. In January 2013 followed 106 (BF62 UYP) and in March came 107 (BV13 ZCZ). Their white livery had Harry Potter vinyls applied.

New premises beckoned as 2013 opened, this time on the Athlon Industrial Estate in

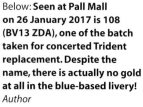

Below: **Seen at Pall Mall on 26 January 2017 is 108 (BV13 ZDA), one of the batch taken for concerted Trident replacement. Despite the name, there is actually no gold at all in the blue-based livery!**
Author

Left: **118 (BU14 EHN) of the 2014 consignment pulls up to Westminster station on 13 February 2017.** *Author*

Wembley. It took a little longer to secure, but occupation began at the end of July.

Open-toppers 108-113 in company blue arrived in April (108-110), May (111, 112) and June (113 and 114); registrations were BV13 ZDA/C-G. The company was becoming so successful that eleven more Volvo B9TLs were ordered in November. These arrived in March 2014 as 114 (BF63 HEJ), a Harry Potter-liveried top-up, followed by part-open-top 115-124 (BF63 HDH/J, BU14 EHM-P/R-T/V) for Trident replacement.

Operations settled; in November 2015 113 gained an ad for Victorinox luggage and a little after that the Harry Potter livery on 105-107 and 114 was updated with a new design. Confidence was high enough to order twenty more buses for 2016; this time they were MCV EvoSeti-bodied Volvo B5TLs and their story can be picked up on page 190.

In April 2016 114 lost its Harry Potter wrap for one advertising The London Ghost Hunters.

Below: **The last of the B9TLs with Golden Tours is 124 (BU14 EHV) and on the afternoon of 13 February 2017 it is seen emerging from Tooley Street at London Bridge.** *Author*

London City Tour

(Various ex-Metroline and London Central)

Below: **On 1 July 2018 BF60 UUG is crossing Westminster Bridge to pick up prospective sightseers. Formerly VW 1849 with Metroline West and still showing that number, it was new to First London as VN 37897 and spent its career in London on the 18.** *Author*

A late entrant to the London sightseeing scene, this firm operated out of a base in Hounslow, later moving to Park Royal, and standardised on Volvo B7TLs, most of which came from the Y-NLK batch of former Metroline VPLs. The company then acquired ex-Abellio, ex-Armchair Tridents, but in 2018 advantage was taken of the large number of very youthful B9TLs returned off lease by Tower Transit. The influx began in January with BF60 UUE (formerly VW 1847 and new as VN 37895), followed in March by BF60 UUC, UUG, UUH and UUJ.

In April came ex-London Central WVLs, LX60 DXC and DXH, with LX60 DWZ in May and LX60 DXA and DXB in June. This batch, were full open-toppers. However, the company closed down after 10 August 2018.

Left: **London City Tours lay over round the back of Waterloo, and on 5 May 2018 we see BF60 UUC pulling in. Formerly Metroline West VW 1846, it began life with First London in 2010 as VN 37894.** *Author*

Below: **The second wave of Volvo B9TLs acquired for replacement of its long-serving ex-Metroline Volvo B7TLs have come from a batch sent off lease by Go-Ahead after just seven years. Coming round Parliament Square on 1 July 2018 with an under-refurbishment Big Ben as a backdrop, LX60 DXH, fully open-top by comparison with the former Metroline West VWs, used to be WVL 377 and spent its short London service career at Bexleyheath.** *Author*

First Berkshire

VNX 37985-37987, 37997-37999

Below: **Looking splendid in First Berkshire's modern interpretation of Green Line livery, Bracknell's VNX 37985 (BJ11 XGY) on 17 June 2012 is almost at the end of another journey from Legoland to Victoria. The buses don't display their class codes, otherwise a quirk of First Berkshire's historical ties with First London.** *Author*

Green Line had been moribund as a brand for years, but First Berkshire was keeping it alive in its own sector through the repainting of a handful of B7TLs cascaded from First London. In mid-2011 three Wrightbus Gemini 2-bodied Volvo B9TLs were ordered to replace coaches that had also been serving on the 702.

The trio arrived in August as VNX 37985-37987 (BJ11 XGY, ECY/X) and were put into service from Bracknell commencing on the the 9th. They occasionally visited local routes 190, 194 and 200.

On 25 November 2012 VNX 37985 was one of the special vehicles run along the Heritage routes 9H and 15H as part of a running day which also saw classic buses on the 24.

Summer 2013 saw three more VNXs ordered to replace one of the four B7TLs drafted in as support. VNXs 37997-37999 (BF63 HDV/X/Y) arrived in October and November and were added to the existing complement. Bracknell closed after 28 August 2015 and the VNXs passed to Slough.

On 27 December 2017 First withdrew from the 702, passing it to Reading Buses.

Left: **The running day held over the Heritage Routes on 25 September 2012 brought VNX 37985 (BJ11 XGY) to the 9H and 15H roads for the first time. During the afternoon it is seen in the company of Ensignbus's roofbox RTL 453 (KLB 648) on the Strand.** *Author*

Left: **VNX 37985 (BJ11 XGY) has finished a journey on the 15H and has segued seamlessly to one on the 9H, helped by adroit programming of the LED blinds. The routes had otherwise been severed when the 9H was rerouted away from Piccadilly Circus and bodily shifted westwards to link High Street Kensington and Trafalgar Square rather than the Royal Albert Hall and Aldwych.** *Author*

Left: **The second batch of Green Line VNXs is seen in the form of VNX 37998 (BF63 HDX) at Hyde Park Corner on 25 May 2017.** *Author*

Ensignbus

111-126, 501-506

Below: **On 8 September 2012 111 (PO58 NPG) pulls into the bus station at Bluewater, carved from the chalk pits in the background.** *Author*

Ensignbus had made its name purchasing the old buses of concerns around the country and world and refitting them for resale, but had bought new for its own concerns comparatively rarely, until 2008, when the company announced an order for ten 10.9m East Lancs (Darwen, and in the event Optare)-bodied Volvo B9TLs for its local network, which was outgrowing its menagerie of Darts. Delivered in the second half of September, nos 111-120 (PO58 NPG/ J/K/N/P/U/V/X/Y, NRE) to H51/31F capacity entered service on the 73 and 83 on 4 September once tree-pruning had been carried out over these routes. One popped up on the X80 in advance and 112 appeared at Showbus on 28 September. As well as their intended routes and regular rail replacement duties, they occasionally visited the 22 and X80, but the 81 much less often.

On 26 April 2011 Ensignbus took on loan a Volvo B5LH hybrid demonstrator registered BK10 MGV; it was cream with green and blue accents and was used on the 73, 83 and X80 for two weeks. While thoughts were entertained of future developments along those lines, the company topped up its existing B9TL fleet with two more second-hand; these were 121 and 122 (PL08 YLZ, YMA) ex-Sanders of Holt and were identical to the indigenous ones other than having high-back seating. 27 December 2011 saw 112 used on First Essex's route 100.

There were indeed to be more Volvo B5LHs, but it was funding from the Green Bus fund that brought them to Ensignbus. The company had already been burned (almost literally!) by the competition when its only recently-acquired ex-Dublin Wrightbus integral 501 took it upon itself to catch fire

Above: **Making good use of its down time on a rail replacement, 111 (PO58 NPG) is seen again, this time at Tower Gateway on 7 July 2013.** *Author*

Left: **Seen on its normal route 22 at Lakeside is 505 (EU62 BYR) on 3 December 2016.** *Author*

Left: **131** *Lance Corporal John Conerly* **(LX15 GVE) was one of the ex-stock Volvo B9TLs taken in 2015, and on 3 December 2016 is seen at Lakeside.** *Author*

and almost take its neighbours with it. The B5LH was a better bet all round, and the five (501-506, registered EU62 BSV/Y, BTF, BYM/R, BVD) arrived between 25 October and November. They were put to use on the 22, already double-decked with acquired Tridents due to demand, and Sunday routes 22A and 73. Capacity was H45/26F.

New route X1 introduced on 3 September 2012 used 121 and 122 and two Enviro400s, all branded specially. June 2013 saw 115 given an orange-based all-over ad for Lakeside and the branding 'theorangebus', which lasted until the following February.

In October 2013 four more B9TLs with the same Optare Olympus 10.9m bodywork (other than one less seat downstairs) were acquired, becoming 123-126 (PO58 KPN/P/R/T). They had been new to Kent Top Travel for the Canterbury Park & Ride.

The newest B9TLs for Ensignbus were five actually stock-built (in white livery) in 2014 but acquired in March 2015 with 15-registrations. 127-131 (LX15 GOK/P/U, GPY, GVE) had Wrightbus Gemini 2-bodied seating 73 (H45/28F) and entered service in the last week of April.

In connection with the company's commemoration of the centenary of the First World War, 26 buses were named after the fallen soldiers commemorated on the war memorial at Purfleet, and the Volvo B9TLs selected to participate were as follows:

115	*Sidney Biles*
118	*Joseph Randall*
119	*Basil Johnston*
120	*Thomas Rowland*
123	*John Suckling*
124	*Edward McKay*
125	*Aldred Godfrey*
126	*John Goldspring*
127	*George Biggs*
128	*John Northmore*
129	*Dugald Campbell*
130	*Archibald Saich*
131	*John Conerly*

Above left: **Second-hand 124** *Private Edward McKay* **(PO58 KPP) is physically identical to Ensignbus's first B9TLs. On 2 December 2017 it is on local route 44 at Lakeside.** *Author*

Left: **Tucking in behind the last of the DMSs, Shillibeer-liveried DM 2646 (THX 646S) on the Ensign running day held on 3 December 2016, B9TL 126** *Private John Goldspring* **(PO58 KPT) leaves Lakeside bus station.** *Author*

Sullivan Buses

WVL 2-4

Long established on the northern fringes of London but without a TfL contract since the loss of the 383 in 2008, Sullivan Buses continued to furnish rail replacements until new contracts were awarded in 2012. On 3 September of that year a spread of school routes commenced, comprising the 628, 653, 683 and 688. Part of their double-deck complement came in the form of WVL 2-4 (FJ57 CYZ, CZD/E), three pre-production Volvo B9TLs with Wrightbus Eclipse Gemini bodywork. They had been new to Wessex Connect and were acquired via Ensign in April. Further school work was won with each new school year, bringing in the 626 in 2013 and the 692 and 699 in 2015. Other than that, appearances on the 298 have been commonplace.

Below: **Rail replacement is the staple work for the three Sullivan Buses Volvo B9TLs when they are not required on their north London school route portfolio. Just such a rail job on 9 August 2015 sees WVL 3 (FJ57 CZD) standing in for the Victoria Line at Seven Sisters.** *Author*

Olympics buses

First 36244-36290 and guests

Below: **First Eastern Counties 36168 (BD11 CFN) combines the Wrightbus Gemini 2 body with the last of the original First 'Barbie' livery as it turns out of the Millennium Busway on 4 August 2012, having finished a run from Charlton station.** *Author*

First offshoot created specifically for the 2012 London Olympic Games is worth including here, as a large component of it was Volvo B9TL-operated. Christened First Games Transport but studiously prohibited from showing any corporate identification, it operated from a First-owned depot in Box Lane, Barking and performed on Park & Rides. Volvo B9TLs 36244-36290 were part of a hundred ordered for Games work before being deployed to West Yorkshire, and sported the new First livery of a rather tamed set of pastel colours. Other B9TLs seconded from First companies across the country continued to carry the old livery and can be compared here.

Left: **Forty-seven B9TLs intended to go into service at First West Yorkshire were seconded to First Games Transport and spent the Olympics on shuttle runs from Charlton to the O2's car park. Showing off the new livery introduced at the time is 36270 (BG12 YKC) on 4 August 2012.** *Author*

Left: **The rear of First's new livery was rather more attractive than the front, for it was only here that you got the intent that it was meant to be a vastly inflated 'f-in'-circle' sign that was carried over from the old branding. 36255 (BG12 YJM) is at the stand ready to leave for another shuttle to Charlton.** *Author*

Left: **Some of the 12-reg B9TLs on Olympic duties carried incorrect numberplates with 'BJ' rather than BG, but 36269 (BG12 YKB) is OK here on the Charlton station shuttle service 22.** *Author*

Go-Ahead

V 6 (i) , V 6 (ii), WVL 509, 510

Below: **The first V 6 (BF63 HFE) is seen in Clayton Road, Peckham, on the morning of 30 October 2013.**
Terry Wong Min

Volvo was continuing to develop its diesel buses, even though the mode was rapidly being supplanted by hybrids, at least in London. Its B5TL came to London in the person of four buses during 2013/14, and two of them, operated by London Central, were known as V 6.

It was also an opportunity to promo the new body, revised by Wrights to reduce the upper-deck window height after complaints about heat ingress. In October 2013 BF63 HFE was taken on loan and put into service on the 12 at Camberwell, numbered V 6. After an unremarkable innings, its spell ended on 21 February 2014 and the bus returned to Volvo in March.

In July 2014 a second V 6 appeared, this time registered BJ14 KTL. Like its predecessor, it was put into service on the 12 out of Camberwell, beginning on 21 August. It heralded the official and rather belated naming of the body as the Gemini 3.

Other than once to the 68 on 15 November, the second V 6 stuck to the 12, and on 26 February 2015 was transferred to Bexleyheath to take its talents to the 229. At the same time London Central was evaluating a Wrightbus Streetdeck integral, numbered WSD 1. Go-Ahead was to take neither Streetdeck nor B5TL, and V 6 returned to Volvo after its last day at Bexleyheath on 24 March.

For the story of the two other B5TLs, which eventually were adopted by Go-Ahead, see pages 188-189.

Arriva

VGD 1

On 23 February 2014 two Volvo B5TLs with Wrightbus Gemini 3 bodywork arrived at Heysham Docks. One of them, BF63 HDE, was for evaluation by Arriva and, following a visit to Metroline (which was expecting the other one; see facing page), it was received by Wood Green on 9 April, numbered VGD 1.

While at Wood Green it was put to work on the W3, commencing on 5 June. It spent July at Volvo's facility at Brimsdown before returning to service on the W3 on 13 August; two trips to the 141 were recorded at the end of 2014. On 2 December it was switched to the 221 and remained working that route until 19 May 2015, after which it was returned to Volvo.

The diesel B5TL had really been eclipsed twofold, first by the Wrightbus Streetdeck, which was taken by Arriva to fulfil its relationship with the manufacturer, and more importantly by the hybrid B5LH, which Arriva London continued to purchase and in increasing numbers. VGD 1 itself subsequently went to Metrobus and was acquired by them as WVL 509 (see page 187).

Below: **VGD 1 (BF63 HDE) spent its first spell at Arriva London North on the W3, switching later to the 221. It is about to commence the climb towards Alexandra Palace on 3 July 2014.** *Terry Wong Min*

Metroline

VW 1469

In May 2014 Metroline took on evaluation Wrightbus Gemini 3-bodied Volvo B5TL BF63 HDG. Numbered VW 1469, this Euro 6-spec diesel bus was allocated to Perivale West and worked on the 297 beginning on 1 August. From 8 December it spread its net wider to cover the 7, 79 and 611 as well as the 297, lasting on these routes until April 2015, when it was returned to Volvo. For its subsequent use by Metrobus, see page 43.

Left: **VW 1469 (BF63 HDG) is seen at Ealing Broadway on 20 November 2014, during its spell on the 297.** *Author*

Left: **13 February has seen VW 1469 (BF63 HDG) taken into town on the 7 to be photographed here at Oxford Circus, but neither deployment prompted repeat orders, Metroline preferring to stick with its tried and trusted B5LH hybrids.** *Author*

Golden Tours

125-144, 201

A lready successful and growing, with a steady input of new buses replacing the Tridents with which it started operations in 2011, Golden Tours ordered 20 MCV EvoSeti-bodied Volvo B5TLs in April 2016. These would follow on from the B9TLs as nos 125-144.

The first of the new buses was in service on 14 May 2016; 125-144 were registered BD16 YEB/C/E-G/J-L/U/V/X/Y, YFA-C/E-H/J. They were joined on 1 June by a B5TL with Wrightbus Eclipse Gemini 3 bodywork, 201 (BD16 YFK), which replaced 114 on the Harry Potter tour. All were in traffic by July.

Below: **MCV EvoSeti-bodied 129 (BD16 YEG) comes past the southern bore of Trafalgar Square on 26 March 2017.** *Author*